McINDOE'S ARMY

The Injured Airmen
Who Faced The World

Peter Williams and **Ted Harrison**

London
PELHAM BOOKS

To Connie
and the Club

First published in Great Britain by PELHAM BOOKS LTD
44 Bedford Square, London WC1
1979

ISBN 0 7207 1191 6

Filmset in Great Britain by
Saildean Limited, Kingston, Surrey
Printed and bound by
Billing & Sons Limited, Guildford

McINDOE'S ARMY

Contents

Illustrations

This book developed from the work and research which Peter Williams and Ted Harrison undertook for a Thames Television documentary *The Guinea Pig Club.*

Reviewers commented on the programme:

'Not the greatest fun' was all one Guinea Pig would say about the total reconstruction of his features. Peter Williams ... managed with a mixture of candour and tact to show his admiration for the club members' special kind of stoicism. But as they grow older, the problems of their disablement inevitably increase. This was a film that was justified in searing the imagination.'

Silvia Clayton in *The Daily Telegraph*

'One of the privileges conferred by extreme suffering is the capacity to be frank, and all concerned unhesitatingly admitted that the battles in the air were an unbeatable thrill. The probability that it takes war to bring out the best in people is hard to accept if your devotion is to peace. Just by letting the heroes talk, this excellent programme raised all the questions.'

Clive James, *The Observer*

'The programme became a tribute to the men themselves. Men who had gone through the severest traumas, involving total disfigurement, loss of sight, loss of limbs, but who had refused to give in, spoke about it all in extreme understatement. Peter Williams and his co-producer Robert Fleming have done us all a great service by demonstrating how un-self-pitying, how humble and yet how noble humanity can sometimes be. It was an uplifting programme.'

Bill Grundy, London *Evening Standard*

Preface

The roll of those whom we wish to thank is as long as the membership list of the remarkable Club – and more. The members and their friends have answered our questions patiently, wittily, poignantly, and never grudgingly.

The programme and this book all began many years ago on a visit to East Grinstead. The discovery that the Guinea Pig Club existed became a fact logged away, an idea for a future documentary film. It was eventually made for Thames in 1979; thanks are also due to them for their permission to use extracts from interviews contained in the programme.

We have many happy memories of our explorations into the Club's affairs over the past forty years. We also mourn the death of actor Edward Chapman and civil engineer Reg Hyde, Guinea Pigs who died in the period during which we were engaged in our research. We know they will be sorely missed.

We wish to thank particularly Tom Gleave and Henry Standen for the hours they spent with us discussing the Club's history and current activities, and to extend our admiration to all those connected with those activities. We hope it is apparent in the pages which follow, all of which were typed with loving care by Jackie Marston.

Finally, we wish to offer our joint sympathy to our families for the experience of living with us during the book's gestation period. It must have been tough.

August 1979

Peter Williams
Ted Harrison

We are McIndoe's Army,
We are his Guinea Pigs.

– from the Guinea Pig Club anthem

1

There's Always Someone Else ...

It is fascinating to identify the corner in which a broken man will find hope. Hope that may grow into interest and then into confidence and, ultimately, into a determination to go on living.

He may find it in religion, or in the love of others, or in a realisation that life, with all it has to offer, is simply too good to let go by default. But among the members of one very special club, hope springs from one harsh, realistic sentence: 'There's always someone worse off than yourself . . . .'

It is the litany of the Guinea Pig Club, even though the members themselves may not realise it, because, if it is anything, it is a club that exists on, and for, mutual support. There is no room for any more hurt; least of all dwelling on the specific details of the misfortunes of another member of the club. Yet time and again, when asked to recall how they climbed out of the lowest troughs in their lives, the moments when they were tempted to cry 'Enough', that sentence bursts into the conversation: 'There's always someone worse off than yourself . . . .'

For the Guinea Pigs, scarred and handicapped by their experiences in the Second World War, it is a Fundamental Truth. Of course, no-one identifies who *is* the Guinea Pig who has been most disfigured by his injuries. In any case, it's very much a matter of opinion. It's enough to believe this Fundamental Truth, to take comfort in it, to wrap around you the knowledge that however difficult it is for you to cope with problems, others have greater injuries

11

and, therefore, greater problems: and they're managing quite well, aren't they?

It was George 'Ben' Bennions who summed it up most graphically. He was one of the early Guinea Pigs; shot down in his Spitfire in 1940, blinded in one eye, half his head shot away. Like all the Guinea Pigs, he came to East Grinstead in Sussex, to the Queen Victoria Hospital. He could still see out of one eye but he was spattered with shrapnel and badly burned. He admits he was feeling sorry for himself. Ben Bennions says:

At the far end of the ward, I saw a badly burned airman in a wheelchair. I'd never seen anyone like it before. He came towards me, propelling his wheel-chair and, as he got closer, I saw that his hands were badly burned and his feet as well. And his ears and his nose. His whole face. It was terrible, really. But, halfway down the ward, he picked up a chair with his teeth. I mean, his lips were badly burned but he caught hold of the back of the chair with his teeth, and he rested the two back legs on the little platform on the front of his wheelchair and he came on towards me, the new boy, at the entrance to the ward.

He stopped beside me, slung the chair off along-side, and he said; 'Have a seat, old boy.'

And I thought: 'What have I got to complain about?' And, from then on, I started to recover.

We talk glibly about the price of war. We think of it in terms of damage and money and death and, of course, human misery. And we welcome the moment when the conflict is over. But these Guinea Pigs, along with the hundreds of thousands of other men injured, physically or mentally, go on paying that price long after the armistice is signed and the guns silenced. They've been paying for it for forty years or more. Those of them who are left are paying it today and will pay it tomorrow, and tomorrow.

In the beginning, there were only a few of them; a few of 'The Few'.

There are seven on the photograph taken with an old box Brownie in 1941 and two of them are already dead. It had all started as a joke. These men, pitifully burned and frequently grossly disfigured, recognised that, in their ability to survive, they were being asked to draw upon special qualities. They recognised, too, that the reconstructive work being carried out at Queen Victoria Hospital was just as special. So, to mark the uniqueness of the whole experience, they decided to formalise their drinking club. Someone had a bottle of sherry, a camera shutter clicked and the Guinea Pig Club was born.

On that July day in Sussex, the new Guinea Pigs chose as their first secretary, Flying Officer Bill Towers Perkins, and as their treasurer, Pilot Officer Peter Weeks. It was an in-joke. Perkins had no hands with which to write minutes; Weeks was unable to walk and therefore could not abscond with the funds.

The members are 'Guinea Pigs' or 'pigs'. The Club's home, Queen Victoria Hospital, is 'the sty'. The Guinea Pigs' children are 'piglets'. The analogy does not extend to the wives of Guinea Pigs.

One of the faces in that early photograph belonged to Geoffrey Page. His appearance was refashioned twice at East Grinstead; once in the early days, once more when, in 1943, he was shot down again. Page recorded the minutes of the first meetings:

The objects of the club are to promote good fellowship among and to maintain contact with approved frequenters of Queen Victoria Cottage Hospital.

There are three classes of membership, all having equal rights:
1   The Guinea Pigs (patients)
2   The Scientists (doctors, surgeons and members of the medical staff)
3   The Royal Society for the Prevention of Cruelty to Guinea Pigs (those friends and benefactors who, by their interest in the hospital

and patients, make the life of a Guinea Pig a happy one).

The annual subscription for all members is 2s 6d. Women are not eligible for membership but a ladies' evening may be held at the direction of the committee. Officers elected:

President: Mr A. H. McIndoe, FRCS; Vice-President: Sqdn Ldr Tom Gleave; Secretary: F/O W. Towers Perkins; Treasurer: P/O P. C. Weeks.

Committee: Messrs Coote, Edmonds, Page, Hughes, Wilton, Overeijnder, Gardiner, Russell Davies, Fraser, Hunter, Eckoff, Morley and Livingstone.

Other members present: Messrs McLeod, Mappin, Clarkson and Bodenham. The following were proposed and seconded as members: Messrs Dewar, Shephard, Lock, Hillary, Fleming, Lord, Hart, Langdale, Bennions, Harrison, Truhlar, Koukall Noble, Mann, Krasnodebski, McPhail, Banham and Smith-Barry.

The Club immediately became the most exclusive in the country, far harder to join, at least as a Category One member, than any of the ancient and privileged haunts of London clubland.

To join as a patient, one had first to be a member of aircrew with the RAF or an Allied Air Force. Very few exceptions were made to this rule. Secondly, one had to be burned, crushed or frost-bitten and require the expert treatment of the plastic and maxillo-facial surgeons. Thirdly, one had to be treated at East Grinstead. To this rule there were *no* exceptions.

That the Club has survived for forty years or so is due to the determination of scores of people interested in the welfare of their fellow human beings. But to understand how the Club has flourished to become what it is today, it's as well to pause to examine the characteristics of three men. Two of them, McIndoe and Russell Davies, are in that original list of names. One, Edward Blacksell, is not. None of them is, or was, aircrew.

The late Sir Archibald Hector McIndoe was born in Dunedin, New Zealand, the grandson of Scottish settlers. For him the road to East Grinstead had led through the Mayo Clinic to a Harley Street practice and a growing specialisation and reputation in the medically unglamorous art of plastic surgery. For him, the war had provided a virtually unlimited supply of pathetic, raw material on which to try the most sophisticated developments in reconstructive surgery, plus a number of new ideas.

It was inevitable, and right, that McIndoe should be the Club's first president. To say that his patients held him in esteem is an understatement. They adored him. Hear Ben Bennions:

He was a god. Really. A remarkable man. Nothing was too much trouble for him when he was caring for the needs of the aircrew he was looking after. He could have got us to do anything.

He hated red tape. He used to cut through it – and that didn't make him popular in Whitehall. He frequently had arguments over his insistence that we, and he, had the facilities that he needed. Once, he threatened that, if he didn't have more money and equipment, he'd mobilise all of us, wheelchairs, crutches, and all, and march us down Whitehall to shame the powers-that-be. We'd have done it for him, too.

Inevitably, McIndoe got what he wanted. But did the men revere McIndoe simply because they needed him and the skill in his short, stubby fingers? 'Yes, that's fair. After all, he was the person putting us back together. He was the recreator, so to speak. Another Good Shepherd, really.' 'Without him, we were lost.'

McIndoe was a practical man. He sustained his Harley Street practice throughout the war, bobbing the nose of a Duchess before travelling to East Grinstead to carry out the fifteenth or twentieth graft to rebuild the face of a fighter pilot, scorched in a manner which came to be known as 'Hurricane Burns'. When he died in April 1960, so successful had he been as a businessman that he left £142,901 – a fortune, even by the City's standards – for, in addition to surgery, McIndoe had had a lucrative hobby: dabbling in stocks and shares.

Like beauty, the quality of a bedside manner lies in the eye of the beholder. Alan Morgan was a Flight Sergeant, a northern lad who'd been an engineering apprentice when he'd joined up. Both his hands were severely frost-bitten, because he'd passed out at altitude, through lack of oxygen, and he hadn't been wearing his gloves. He remembers his first impression of McIndoe. The surgeon had been in the habit of visiting other hospitals to vet the worst cases before taking them to East Grinstead and into his care.

McIndoe got me from the hospital in Colchester and put my hands in ice buckets. I was like that for ten days. When they came out of the ice buckets they were in bandages. The tips of the fingers were all black, just like little sticks of black. They kept on bandaging them up, and having another look, and I must have been a month like that. Just hoping. And then, one day, McIndoe came and sat on the bed and he said;

'Right, Alan. We'll have to take them off. You're due for the chop.'

He said it in a joking manner. But I knew he was serious. And I also knew he'd do something good for me. Because I'd seen what he'd done for the other lads. How he'd made their hands. And I knew he'd make the best of a bad job. Which he did.

McIndoe removed all Alan Morgan's fingers, but saved his thumbs. In saving his thumbs, he saved his ability to grip. And in saving that, he rescued for Alan Morgan the ability to do the only job he'd ever wanted to do – to be an engineer; which he's done successfully ever since.

Richard Hillary, caustic, self-assured, intellectual,

author of *The Last Enemy,* a moving chronicle of his experiences as a pilot bady-burned on face and hands, remembers McIndoe coming to see him at the Masonic Hospital:

> Of medium height, he was thick-set and the line of his jaw was square. Behind his horn-rimmed spectacles a pair of tired, friendly eyes regarded me speculatively.
>
> 'Well,' he said, 'you certainly made a thorough job of it, didn't you?'
>
> He started to undo the dressings on my hands and I noticed his fingers – blunt, capable, incisive. He took a scalpel and tapped lightly on something white showing through the red, granulating knuckle of my right forefinger.
>
> 'Bone,' he remarked laconically.

McIndoe was frank with his patients about the treatment they would have to undergo and they were grateful to him for that. In this relationship, familiarity bred respect. Sam Gallop, who lost both his legs when his plane crashed, remembers:

> It was always 'Sir' with McIndoe. People now say 'Archie' in a sort of fond remembrance but, at the time, he was in a very human way, The Boss. And that was the right way to run the ship and he wouldn't – or maybe couldn't – run it any other way.
>
> But, at the same time, he had this way of creating a wonderful relaxed atmosphere, in which people could regain their own personalities. I mean, you could call the nurses by their Christian names. Now that doesn't sound very dramatic – but at that time it was. And for me it was a novel experience.
>
> Remember, I'd just come from an Air Force hospital where, despite the fact I had no legs, I'd been told to lie to attention because a senior RAF medical officer was making the rounds. . . .

But it would be an exaggeration to suggest that the Guinea Pig Club has developed along lines forseen by a wise Archibald McIndoe. In the early days McIndoe quite properly saw his task simply as getting the injured aircrew fit so that they could fly again. The Club set a seal on the cameraderie that already existed among the young men who were hospitalised for months on end. It was only later that, in his mind and in the minds of others, there grew the realisation of a gap that needed to be filled, a need that had to be met; a job, in short, for the Guinea Pig Club to do.

One of the other faces caught and preserved by the box Brownie in that photograph of 1941 is that of Dr Russell Davies. At the time he was number two among McIndoe's anaesthetists. Number one, 'the Knock-Out King', the man whose reputation as 'a wizard with the gas works' was matched only by his reputation as the most generous man in East Grinstead, was Dr John Hunter. Hunter was a massive, ebullient, expansive man, who could drink any Guinea Pig under the table. While McIndoe often had a private arrangement with publicans in the town that when he asked for a gin he was given harmless tonic water, John Hunter had no qualms about drinking and socialising and still keeping a clear head for the morning to start work on McIndoe's list.

Russell Davies worked beside John Hunter, as his junior partner until the early 1950s, when he assumed his mantle. Hunter, the high-liver, was also a diabetic, and he died young and suddenly.

For almost forty years, Russell Davies has listened to the Guinea Pigs' problems. He's assessed their needs and how best to meet them, in partnership with a man who didn't join the Club until 1942, Edward Blacksell.

'Blackie' Blacksell was to become headmaster of Barnstaple Secondary School in North Devon, a director of the English Stage Company at the Royal Court Theatre, and a consultant at Sotheby's in London; in 1942, he was a lanky RAF physical training instructor. It is difficult to fathom the line of reasoning that led, first to school teacher

Blacksell becoming a PTI and second, to a PTI being posted to a hospital where most of the inmates were incapable of anything but the most carefully-monitored movements, particularly when undergoing treatment. But it happened, and Blackie became what may best be described as a welfare officer for the Club and the patients. No one listens to them more sympathetically. With Davies, and drawing on their forty years' experience, he understands the nuances of the situations presented to him, the words left unsaid.

From the beginning, the Club has met regularly. Now, it's once a year, in September, a hotel near East Grinstead for a dinner and dance, and a series of events spread over the weekend, the Lost Weekend as it's always been known. Why 'Lost'? Largely because of the amount of alcohol consumed (admittedly by a minority) and the blurring of memory that may result.

During the course of that weekend, in a room at the hospital, Russell Davies and Edward Blacksell sit and wait and listen. And the Guinea Pigs bring their problems: social problems that are Blackie's speciality; medical and disablement problems that Russell Davies knows about, financial problems for them both to ponder over. And throughout the weekend, at the cocktail party beside the hospital swimming pool, at the annual darts match at the red-brick pub near the hospital which has been named The Guinea Pig, you overhear the snatches of conversation . . . .

'We'll have one of the surgeons take a look at that eyelid . . . . '

'That ear doesn't look too happy. Is it giving you any trouble . . . . '

'And if the pension people give you any bother just let me know . . . . '

Almost forty years on, forty operations later, this is one of the unpublicised prices of victory. Thankfully, most of the battles on behalf of the Guinea Pigs, in which Blackie and Russell Davies – and earlier, McIndoe himself – were involved have also ended in victory for the Club: the fight,

in the early days, for a proper level of disability pension
for the injured airmen; the forging of the links with the
RAF Benevolent Fund, whose sympathetic response to
appeals for help over the years has solved so many Guinea
Pigs' practical problems, and prevented many of them
plumbing the depths of despair. And, putting money
aside, there are the victories that meant so much to
morale. There's the Battle of the Blues, which Blackie
remembers, being fought soon after he arrived.

> The issue was very simple. The Air Ministry said: 'If
> you are injured, you must wear "hospital blues", a
> standard blue uniform with a red tie and a white
> shirt.' The Guinea Pigs said: 'We don't want to wear
> that comic opera uniform for months on end. We're
> aircrew and we're proud of it.'
>   They were proud of their insignia, their wings
> – and that was understandable. So one night, they
> burned some 'hospital blues', which reaped an
> immediate reaction from the Air Ministry. RAF
> Regiment policemen appeared mysteriously in the
> town. All personnel were to wear proper uniform
> and, if that was 'hospital blues', then the Guinea Pigs
> must wear 'hospital blues' . . . .
>   The battle was won by a stroke of genius. The
> 'proper uniform' for sporting activities was sports
> gear. So, with McIndoe's blessing, the Guinea Pigs,
> halt, lame and lazy, wore sports kit and, when asked,
> politely replied that they were on the way to the
> tennis lawns or the swimming pool or the running
> track . . . .

The issue of 'hospital blues' was never again raised,
though, typically, McIndoe retained the threat of a spell in
'hospital blues' as a disciplinary measure, to keep some of
his livelier Guinea Pigs in line!
    Over the years Russell Davies has led the negotiations
with various authorities over the proper recognition a
grateful nation should make to its injured warriors by way

of a pension. He's been helped by another of McIndoe's quirks – a willingness to allow Guinea Pigs to see the operations they were about to undergo. Frequently the gallery in the hospital theatre was full of Guinea Pigs and visiting surgeons and doctors, all there to watch McIndoe at work. The fact that the Guinea Pigs knew and understood what was happening to them during the series of operations was to prove 'extraordinarily helpful', says Davies, 'when preparing a case to argue'.

Russell Davies now lives in Winchester but, in many senses, his life still centres on East Grinstead. He is a thoughtful, quietly spoken Welshman. He has a wry smile that turns aside the important question. When John Hunter died, McIndoe wanted Davies to come into his private practice. It was a lucrative offer but Davies refused. Was it because he felt a man could not properly serve both the National Health Service and private practice? Was it because he felt that someone, somebody from the 'old team', must stay at East Grinstead, to be there when the Guinea Pigs needed them? Again, the wry smile. . . .

But there is no doubt that Russell Davies feels an on-going concern, a degree of responsibility for each of the six hundred or so members of the Club. He knows he has administered anaesthetic to some Guinea Pigs forty or fifty times. He wonders about the effect that this, and the series of operations, has had on their constitution. He puts it this way:

I'd rather be 'under' for half an hour than for two hours. I'd rather have one operation, than four. I'd rather have five than eight; ten than twenty.

I believe we've all been given so much ... courage, for want of a better word. And each time we go through an ordeal like this, we draw on our deposits of courage. Some of these men, some of my friends, had drawn heavily on their courage before they came to us. Simply in surviving the experience of crashing, I mean. I'm determined, and so are the rest of the

Club, that if and when they need any support, that
support won't be lacking.

The support, over the years, has come from men such as
Russell Davies, Blackie Blacksell and Bernard Arch, an
RAF Corporal posted to the hospital, who has given many
thousands of dedicated hours as the Club's secretary.
There's Chief Guinea Pig Tom Gleave, who was shot
down and, as he puts it, 'fried' in 1940; Guinea Pig Henry
Standen, the Guinea Pig magazine editor, and his wife
Ann, who was a nurse at the hospital and now helps
organise the dinner every year. And help comes from the
Guinea Pigs themselves, who perhaps know the problems
best. Blackie is very frank about the problems, and about
the difficulties they caused.

These were, vigorous, bright and, usually, handsome
young men transformed in an instant into A Problem – a problem for others but, most importantly, to
themselves.
  How were they going to cope? Most of them had
never even seen the faces or the hands of a badly
burned man, let alone thought about what it would
be like to be one.
  How were they going to work? To eat? How were
they going to attract a pretty girl? How were they
going to manage courtship, making love? We picked,
incidentally, the prettiest nurses we could find to
work at East Grinstead – and I didn't hear too many
complaints either from the patients or the nurses.
  We tried to place the men in jobs and, though
many of the firms were sympathetic, they hadn't the
faintest idea of what these young men needed. After
all, they were fit young men, who'd simply been
disfigured. One firm offered a number of jobs as
liftmen. Now, how could you ask a squadron leader
to become a liftman? And one very famous retail
store in London expressed an eager interest in
placing the Guinea Pigs in proper employment – but

once they'd met one of the Guinea Pigs they contacted us and said:

'We'd love to help. But could you please arrange for the men to wear some kind of a mask.'

Now how can you begin to convince a man that he may once more take his place in society, if his employer will give him a job only if he hides his face?

Right from the early days, we've been certain that the most important task for the Club has been to see that every member recognises and retains his own essential dignity. We've been determined that no member of the Guinea Pig Club shall, as it were, be seen selling matches from a tray on the street corner.

And that, Chief Guinea Pig Tom Gleave proudly boasts, has never happened. 'And we would move heaven and earth if we ever found it happening.' He pauses. 'In fact, the biggest single achievement of the Guinea Pig Club is to have helped every member to save his face. His "other" face, that is, in a psychological sense, so that he could securely take his place once more in society.'

Among these men – Blackie, Russell Davies and, before his death, McIndoe – there is a real respect, a love, for those injured airmen. It shows in big ways, in their commitment to them, and in small ways that you'll notice during a moment's pause during the Lost Weekend. For, make no mistake, this is the Guinea Pigs' Club. Ultimately, they call the tune, they make the decisions. On at least one occasion, they disagreed with McIndoe and out-voted him. On reflection, McIndoe would have smiled about this, for it proved how successful he and the Club were becoming in their self-appointed task of restoring the men's self-confidence and self-respect – in short saving that 'other' face.

Archibald McIndoe

2

Ward Three

Just to the left as you face the old hospital at East Grinstead there are some temporary buildings. Like so many temporary buildings they have been there a long time and, patched and painted, have given around forty years of service. The main building of the group is a hut. It's known as Ward Three.

Inside Ward Three there have been a few changes since the war; the old Ministry of Works colour scheme, dark green and cream, has been painted over and brightened; the beds are, perhaps, more spaced out; the old coke stove has gone; the grand piano, which McIndoe would play, has also been moved and there is no longer a barrel of beer on tap. Nor is there a curious Heath Robinson contraption, a large bath with pipes, buckets, lights and bells to be seen: the saline bath devised by the surgeon to enable a burned man to rest in healing, saline water maintained at blood heat, an innovation which proved so popular and restful for the Guinea Pigs that some would try to stay hours in the water just resting and reading.

Physically, apart from those specific changes, things in the ward are very much as they were. But a Guinea Pig would notice one marked difference. The atmosphere of the ward has changed completely. There is nothing in Ward Three today which would distinguish it from any other ward in any other hospital in Britain.

Almost forty years ago there was nowhere in Britain quite like Ward Three. Flight Sergeant Alan Morgan came from a hospital in Chichester to East Grinstead for

25

treatment to his frost-bitten hands. His first impression of
the ward was that it was like a mad house.

> It wasn't a hospital, it was just a big comfortable
> hotel. It was mad, everybody was doing their own
> thing. There was a big barrel of beer at the end of the
> ward and you could help yourself. They called it 'the
> barrel of beer which never ran dry . . . . ' People were
> coming and going all the time. At that time, I didn't
> want to be bothered by anybody, I just wanted to be
> quiet. But people would come in and they would be
> drunk, and it would make no difference and they
> would go to their beds relatively quietly, and only
> later did I notice that they were all far more badly
> injured than I was.
>   The nurses were fantastic. We had a lot of time
> between operations. I might come in from an even-
> ing in London at a show and I would have had a
> scotch or two. But it never bothered the nurses. They
> would just say, 'Well, would you like some toast and
> dripping?' and they would make your supper and
> they would get you back to bed with as little fuss as
> possible and that was how it was.

Hardly the accepted image of a military hospital in
wartime.

For his first impressions of Ward Three, Pilot Officer
Jimmy Wright had to rely solely on his hearing. He had
been blinded in a crash in Italy. It was 1944. He had been
flown back at the insistence of his father through some of
the most dangerous air routes in Europe. He had even
needed an escort of Spitfires to arrive in Britain safely. For
Jimmy Wright, encountering the noise in Ward Three was
like a physical shock:

> There was somebody ticking away at a typewriter,
> learning to type, and radios were going and there was
> general noise and chaos, and I wished that I was back
> in the quiet hospital in Italy.

I met The Boss, Archibald McIndoe, two or three days after my arrival. The first thing that had happened was that I had a brine, a saline, bath to ease the burns on my legs and hips. I think it was about five o'clock in the afternoon, after he had finished his day's surgery, and I had a lot of pain in the right eye and he took one look at it and said that he would operate that night. It was certainly a relief the next day to have the eye covered and have less pain, though I was a little surprised to find myself in the operating theatre so suddenly.

Jimmy Wright was at East Grinstead for four years. It was not a continuous stay, as it was not wise to subject a patient to continuous surgery for more than a three or four month period.

We looked upon East Grinstead as a sort of country club. It was rather like coming home. I suppose I was in hospital for such a long time that I made a lot of friends locally. And, of course, there were the chaps who were in the ward with me, who were coming and going in the same way. In a sense I had more friends at East Grinstead than at my home, because I had lost several of my close friends during the war.

Bill Simpson is not a man who takes easily to an atmosphere of bonhomie and cheerful comradeship; still less when he was grievously injured in the early stages of the war. In some ways he feels that McIndoe, in creating the atmosphere he did at East Grinstead, went too far. He had two years at the hospital. He wrote at the time:

Cheerfulness invaded the consciousness of even the most unreceptive patients. Firstly, the patients were brothers in misfortune, a community of people who had all, and were all suffering in the same way. Secondly, whereas most of the patients were grotesque in appearance, the nurses were nearly all very pretty.

Nurses, incidentally, applying for jobs at East Grinstead had to send a photograph of themselves for The Boss's approval. His idea was that all the nurses had to be able to communicate with, and relate to, the patients underneath their scars, injuries and dressings. They nursed them as young virile men and not as broken war-wounded. A third factor in the fashioning of an atmosphere, Simpson observed, was the interest shown by the outside community. Many East Grinstead citizens visited the ward, took patients out, and in the town itself the patients were welcomed. It was as if East Grinstead had taken a corporate decision to help the men as part of their war effort.

But perhaps the greatest contribution to the atmosphere of the ward emanated from McIndoe himself. 'To him we are human beings first and patients second. He jokes with us in the ward and sometimes when we lie on the operating table; he will drink with us in the town; he enjoys life; he is one of us.'

McIndoe's right hand man in all things non-medical was Edward Blacksell, Blackie.

Ward Three was like a very jolly sixth form room or undergraduate common room just before the Christmas vacation. This was quite deliberate. There were no rules and regulations. If you felt like getting out of bed, you got out of bed. If you felt like having a drink, you had a drink. If you felt like chatting up the nurses, you were encouraged to do so; and by the way we had some remarkable nurses which we chose with great care, partly because they were very beautiful and partly because they were knowledgeable in the sense of knowing how to cope with fresh young men.

We chose beautiful nurses as an encouragement to people who had been grossly disfigured and particularly those who had bad hand disfigurement. We had to prepare the nurses very carefully for the specific and rather special job of nursing that they were going into.

Their job was to make a man feel presentable and needed and also to prevent the patients from over-doing things. It wasn't just a problem with the shy and disillusioned: we had problems with the over stressed extrovert as well.

Arguably, no one is now closer to the Guinea Pigs than Blackie. It is a family bond. He feels he belongs to the Guinea Pigs; he feels responsible for them and totally involved in their world. He has shared their more riotous moments, once being 'debagged', and their times of despair.

I know of no way of minimising that terrible despair that comes upon a patient, say, at three o'clock in the morning, when nothing has gone right and his graft has sloughed off, when he feels there is no more skin left to be grafted, when his girl friend has left him, when he's made a hash of something and he sees no future in front of him and he's alone in bed, other than by just happening to be around.

I remember saying to one Guinea Pig that if he wanted to end it all, if he really wanted to do that, then I'd not stop him. He's still alive today.

There were obviously some very desperate moments. Yet even at moments of greatest despair we believed it would have been wrong to shelter Guinea Pigs from the reality of their disabilities. They knew as early as possible that they had no fingers. In my time, there were always mirrors about so that they could see what they looked like; they met Guinea Pigs who were further advanced from a surgical point of view, because there was always somebody who had been through the machine before you.

Bertram Owen Smith came to Ward Three early in

November 1941. By the time he joined, he had accepted that he would be in hospital sometime. From Darlington he was moved further south to Lincolnshire. There, Archibald McIndoe, on one of his 'scouting missions', saw him and arranged for him to be taken to East Grinstead. His first feeling in Ward Three was one of relief. He saw a room full of men suffering in various degrees from severe burns. He was not alone. He liked the atmosphere of freedom and camaraderie. And there was no room for self-pity:

> The old hands treated me very scathingly. They would walk up and assess you, give you a look over and conclude, 'Och, you've just been singed'. That quickly stopped you feeling sorry for yourself. You realised very quickly that no matter how bad you thought you were, there were always chaps who were ten times worse.

Despite the easy atmosphere, there was discipline. Owen Smith continues:

> If you knew that you were due to go on 'the slab' the next morning, as the operating table was called, then you didn't go down to town. You didn't have a few beers.
> You maintained, quite voluntarily, the basic disciplines required to run a ward. Anyone who contravened them was censured by the chaps themselves. They wouldn't allow one person to spoil the freedom we all enjoyed.

McIndoe himself claimed that the ward had only two unbreakable rules: one, don't touch my nurses; two, don't touch my daughters. Even so, these rules were not always kept. After all, apart from their scars, there were a lot of perfectly healthy men in the ward with all the ordinary appetites of youth. One Guinea Pig remembers being disturbed one night by a strange banging noise. He investigated and found a theatre trolley bearing the recumbent bodies of a nurse and patient, thumping rhythmically against the wall of a corridor.

Many patients married their nurses. As Bertram Owen Smith remembers: 'While you were mobile, between operations, you could go into East Grinstead and a lot of chaps arranged to meet nurses or girls from the town there. I think it was even part of the treatment, as McIndoe recognised it.'

For Geoffrey Page, Ward Three was a 'cross between Emergency Ward 10, The Red Lion and a French bordello.' It was a place of fun. For there is a vast difference between a ward where you have injured people and a hospital where you have sick people.

If someone was incredibly ill, you didn't disturb them. It was an unwritten law that you left him alone and if the ward sister or nurse said, 'Look he's having a rough time', we tiptoed around. But the moment he was all right, we'd pour beer over him. That was part of the rehabilitation process.

[Did this mean that Guinea Pigs were in general hard and unsympathetic?] It is true they revelled in black humour. They were irreverent and even earned the rebuke from a local clergyman that they were the most ungodly people he had ever come across. The operating table was always known as 'the slab' and an operation was 'going under the knife'. They would refer to the experience of being burned as being 'fried'. But they reserved sympathy for genuine cases. And they decided who were the genuine cases. Someone who felt sorry for himself was quickly brought into line.

Patients were allowed to watch McIndoe at work in the operating theatre. To begin with, this was a rather crowded affair in the small theatre in the old cottage hospital building. Later, when the new wing was built, the theatres were given observation galleries. All Guinea Pigs were expected to have a basic knowledge of the medical implications of their own treatment, so that McIndoe could discuss his ideas and suggestions with them. There were other surgeons at the hospital and East Grinstead often attracted visiting specialists. Guinea Pigs quickly formed their own impressions of the other surgeons and were quite ready to criticise them. No visiting surgeon could afford to be off-hand in his bedside approach. Guinea Pigs wanted to know exactly what was going to happen to them; they felt it was their right to be consulted.

Tom Gleave recalls that with McIndoe there was no question of a superior being making decisions the patients could not understand. 'You were just two people in Ward Three, one waiting on the other, and this was the magic. You knew exactly what he was going to do to you, but you got the impression he was asking your advice.'

It would be wrong to suggest that McIndoe was able to control a complete ward through the strength of his personality alone. He had spells away from the hospital, sometimes quite long ones, scouring the military hospitals around the country for new cases and dealing with his private practice. He had therefore to have certain sanctions. The ultimate sanction was that a patient would be transferred from East Grinstead to another, more traditional, service hospital. This happened no more than once or twice. The other sanction was that a patient could be made to dress in one of the few sets of hospital blues which had escaped the bonfire at the Queen Victoria hospital. It is a mark of the success of the self-regulating system of discipline that only three or four patients were ever made to wear the despised blues.

Over the years the atmosphere in Ward Three gradually changed. Early on in the war McIndoe's patients were the élite, the heroes of the Battle of Britain. He was able to give them far more personal attention than later, when the number of injured men grew considerably. It was The Few, in the early days, who created the spirit of the ward, but it could be maintained only through some form of mutually acceptable discipline. McIndoe was pragmatic. He used the Club to achieve his objectives. The hospital grew. It began to treat large numbers of Canadians and a special Canadian wing was built. There were other nationalities as well as men from the other Services. But membership of the Guinea Pig Club was, with very few exceptions, restricted to air crew. Yet the spirit of the Club spread generally through the hospital.

Members of the Guinea Pig Club are, almost without exception, above the average in intelligence. They had to be exceptional to be selected for flying duties. The early Guinea Pigs were generally from public school and university backgrounds; the majority of the later members were from more middle- and working-class backgrounds. But they have all benefited from the orderly way in which the Club developed during the war and after it. As Secretary Bernard Arch says today: 'We were working to form a blueprint to tackle human problems of a type, and on a scale, never faced before.'

Not all Guinea Pigs were required to be in hospital all the time. There would be long rests from operations when Guinea Pigs would be able to go to Marchwood Park in Hampshire or Saint Hill Manor near East Grinstead where there were workshops. Not basket weaving or rug making. Guinea Pigs were involved in the manufacture of items for aircraft navigation and produced articles of the very highest standard. The intricate work which they were often required to do was invaluable in producing new skills and letting Guinea Pigs rediscover how to use their hands. On one official tour of the workshops, a VIP asked a Guinea Pig how they managed, with deformed hands, to produce work of a consistently higher standard than other factories where able-bodied people were working. He was told in no uncertain manner that airmen's lives depended on their work. They needed no greater motivation.

Ward Three was nothing if not democratic. There was none of the normal segregation of a service hospital. There could be a Lance Corporal in one bed and an Air

Marshal on the other side. There was mutual tolerance and respect. Indeed the story is told of McIndoe, for ever the opportunist, conceiving some of his earlier ideas for Ward Three from the observation that officers, segregated in private wards alone, tended to recover at a slower rate than the men in the communal wards.

Bill Warman became a Guinea Pig when the Club had already been established and the hospital was in full swing. 'There was a lot of fun there, but don't let me give the impression it interfered with the efficiency of the place, because it didn't.'

Over the years the memories of the high-jinks in East Grinstead have rather overshadowed the memories of pain, fear and self-discipline. Stories abound of traffic signs being uprooted in the town and brought back to the hospital; wheelchair races down a nearby hill and the revelry of drunken parties. There's the one about the Guinea Pig who kept a car in East Grinstead. He took it into the centre of the town and parked it outside a pub. He went inside, leaving the car blocking one lane of traffic. Before long, a traffic jam built up and a policeman was given the job of clearing the obstruction. He went into the pub and made some enquiries and soon discovered the owner, propping up the bar with a drink in his hand. With the full majesty of the law behind him, the policeman asked the Guinea Pig: 'Why have you left your car outside the pub, sir?'

'Because', replied the Guinea Pig, 'the car doesn't drink.'

By the standards of the day Ward Three was remarkable in its approach. Sam Gallop, the man without legs, who was told to lie to attention on his bed in another service hospital of the day, describes the Ward Three atmosphere as very professional. 'There were very tight medical rules, but at the same time a wonderful balance of being relaxed. There was leg-pulling amongst patients which was quite unique in my experience and a very good approach to rehabilitation. But it was a very tight medical ship.' His immediate reaction to Ward Three was 'curiosity, amused curiosity, intrigued curiosity, to find, for example, that there was a bar. There weren't great drinkers or anything but there was a bar and this was, to put it mildly, rather unusual.'

As the weeks became months, Gallop believes that those who settled best were slightly schizophrenic.

I think all of us were obliged to be detached. There were always two of each of us. The person this was happening to, who was very much involved, and could feel things very strongly, and the observer just watching and assessing. I think it was a necessary defence to preserve this other person who had an element of detachment. One couldn't afford to care about oneself too much. It wasn't constructive. If you cared about yourself too much you were liable to get the wind up about the next operation, wonder whether it would succeed or not, wonder where the hell you were going to be at the end of eighteen months and so on, and one really had to live from five minutes to five minutes. We were encouraged to do that because there were no false hopes, no false dreams. It was going to be an unpleasant time and we were given every support to get through this. But you could not afford to get too emotionally involved about it.

One of the nurses at East Grinstead was Jean Fuggle. With her application for the post at the hospital she was asked to send a photograph. Being an attractive young woman with considerable nursing experience, she got the job. She came from completing a course in tropical medicine in London and was interested in learning about a new area of nursing. She arrived on her first day at the Canadian Wing and remembers walking through a ward. She was moved by what she saw but not shocked. After all, she had dealt with amputation cases and other severe injuries suffered by people who had been injured in the blitz. Even if she had felt emotionally torn by seeing these disfigured young men for the first time, she was not going to be allowed to brood. There was a party going on. She was immediately invited to join in.

She remembers genuine amazement when invited to the operating theatre. She found herself surrounded by Guinea Pigs, watching the surgery. The first operation involved replacing a nose. She was intrigued that patients had such courage to watch McIndoe explaining the operation they themselves would be having within a few days.

McIndoe's frequently quoted ambition was to return every patient to a full and active life as a worthwhile member of the community. Merely stating this as an ambition was part of the cure. No Guinea Pig was allowed to conclude that his life was to be of no value. They were encouraged, urged to face the world again. But one particular visit temporarily undermined McIndoe's work. A group of Guinea Pigs was taken to Buckingham Palace to a garden party. On the way back, they were all very subdued. After persistent questioning Blackie got to the root of the problem. It seemed the Guinea Pigs had been left for the afternoon with a group of veterans from the First World War; old men from the Star and Garter home. Many of them were badly injured, but in their day, there had been no McIndoe to save them or their self-respect. They had been 'tucked away' in a home where the public would not see them again. The Guinea Pigs had sensed that their own future might be in doubt if this was the public attitude towards them. They were disfigured as well; might they be pushed kindly aside into an institution? It is difficult to reassure men as deeply hurt as fledgeling Guinea Pigs.

Fortunately this was an isolated case. At the outset McIndoe had sought the co-operation of East Grinstead, going around East Grinstead explaining his ideas and asking for the townspeople's help. It worked. Spontaneously, the Guinea Pigs now describe East Grinstead, in a phrase borrowed from some long-forgotten newspaper article, as the 'town that never stared'.

The Guinea Pigs' favourite haunt was the Whitehall, a pub-cum-restaurant-cum-cinema complex in the centre of the town. Under the kindly and tolerant eye of the manager, Bill Gardiner, the Pigs were able to regain their social confidence.

At first, a new boy might hide his face behind his hands and sit by himself in a corner, but gradually he would 'peep out through his fingers and then show his face until he was quite at ease', which is how Mabel Osborne, one of the waitresses, and Sue Berjeaux, the cook, remember it. McIndoe's carefully formed tubes of flesh, pedicles, which he used to raise skin for grafting from one part of the body to another, were called 'sausages', by Mabel. 'Even with a sausage coming down from the nose and one hand bandaged up, they managed to eat and drink, though sometimes we had to cut their food up for them.'

The Guinea Pigs were always careful to ask McIndoe not to operate on both hands at the same time. One hand had to be free for use. Some Guinea Pigs would give the surgeon lists of things they wanted done, 'shopping lists' which they would pin to themselves before an operation. Often McIndoe would see the list, tick each item as he completed it, or explain why he was not able to fulfil the request.

In all, about 640 airforce personnel became Guinea Pigs. During the war, the hospital continued to serve the local community and McIndoe and his team were there when needed after a German bomb fell on the Whitehall cinema, killing and injuring scores of citizens of East Grinstead.

But none of these extra patients became Guinea Pigs. The exclusiveness of the Club was maintained. Though there is no such thing as a 'typical' Guinea Pig, they do have an astonishing, almost telepathic, group will, which Russell Davies remarks upon. At the Lost Weekend, if a guest speaker is not to their liking, the collective opinion of the Guinea Pigs can swamp him like a tidal wave. He's seen it happen. One year, the Guinea Pigs took an instant and inexplicable dislike to a speaker. 'If he had spoken a moment longer, and as luck had it he was very brief, there would have been a riot,' Russell Davies recalls.

Not all Guinea Pigs attend the annual weekends. Some come every other year, others have perhaps only attended once or twice. But there is a hard core of regulars and every year, in total, more than one hundred Guinea Pigs from all over the world get together.

Henry Standen now lives within a mile of the hospital; he regained the use of his hands and has contributed cartoons to Punch. Noel Newman wanted to be a surgeon; he lost the mobility in his hands and became medical officer of health at Bath. Then there are the two film stars: Bill Foxley, who played the injured pilot in the highly successful film, *The Battle of Britain,* and Jack Allaway whose face was reconstructed so well that he was given the starring role in a short film about East Grinstead made by the Canadians. Tubby Taylor, lively irrepressible Taylor, rounds off every weekend by leaping, fully clothed, into the swimming pool at the hospital. And there are so many others, who come year after year. So many stories ...

We have chosen just a few to write about in detail. For this is a book which could have as many chapters as there are members. What follows forms, we hope, a cross-section of the stories of the remarkable men who make up this remarkable Club.

3

Tom Gleave

Chief Guinea Pig seems a curious title for a grown man to cherish, but to a select group of men it is a title of honour and responsibility. Tom Gleave, the current Chief Guinea Pig, never shirks the responsibility, nor loses sight of the honour.

He works from a small office in his home at Bray, alongside the River Thames, as an official historian of the Second World War. But at any moment his telephone may ring and Tom Gleave can find himself springing into action on behalf of a Guinea Pig with a problem. Officially the Club has a healthy disregard for paper and red tape. Unofficially, Gleave's spare room is its headquarters, and a cupboard full of files and papers its administrative block.

Tom Gleave was present at the birth of the Club. He was one of The Few at the sherry party at the hospital that Sunday morning in July 1941, who decided that the comradeship which had grown out of the common experience of suffering should not be left to die. Gleave calls those beginnings 'a grogging club' – an occasion for drinking. But by 1945 the Club had become a registered charity. Its constitution, aims and objects were recorded and its officers listed. Among those, as vice-president, was Tom Gleave, later to succeed McIndoe as Chief Guinea Pig.

The Club's rules, written or unwritten, are very simple. The aim is to enable Guinea Pigs to keep in touch with each other, and with the doctors, surgeons, nurses and other friends, who are always willing to help them. At the

Tom Gleave

centre of the club's activities is the Lost Weekend, an opportunity for any Guinea Pig to, using Sir Archibald McIndoe's phrase, 'recharge his batteries'. To many Guinea Pigs the Weekend has become less of the long drinking session that it used to be and more of the opportunity to catch up on news and views. The Lost Weekend has survived the passing years while many regimental or squadron reunions have faded away.

It's a time for nostalgia. While a whole generation has grown up without any idea of what war is like, and many people who lived through the war have put it out of their minds, the Guinea Pigs cannot forget. Their scars and disabilities are a constant reminder. 'War', says Tom Gleave, 'is a horrible shocking thing. But there are facets to a war which bring out the best in people. Lots of people in the war were utterly unselfish and incredibly brave. They had a cause. There is something indefinably grand about battle. It captivates the people, even those who take part in it.'

That is why people will go on reading about the Battles of Waterloo and Trafalgar for ever, maintains Gleave, the historian. 'In a story like the Battle of Britain, you have this fantastic back-drop which we had never seen before and may never see again; it was grand to be there. I haven't met a chap yet, whether he's been burnt or pulled to pieces or not, who would have missed that for all the tea in China. It was quite terrific.'

Historian he may be, but he doesn't live in the past. Yet his memories of the Battle of Britain are still vivid. The air was full of lead. Imagine he says eighty multi-gun fighters firing from all different angles; in the middle, the bombers with six or eight guns each firing as well. Yet he was not gripped by fear. His main emotion was anger – anger that those 'bloody Germans' were flying over his country. He did not think of the man flying at him as a person. If he had been shot down, baled out and been captured and they had met on the ground, he says, he would probably have taken him to the mess and given him a beer. But in the skies above southern England and the Channel it was

quite different. 'You are in the shop up there. You are
selling stuff over the counter – death. And God help the
poor sod who bought it.'

Tom Gleave still remembers the moment *he* nearly
bought it. He remembers his struggle to open the hood of
the burning aircraft and the explosion which shot him
through a sheet of flames. He remembers pulling the rip
cord of his parachute and floating down to earth a very
angry man.

It was a beautiful hot day, the weather was hazy and
the roads below him were shimmering. Mingling with
the anger in his mind were some strange inconsequen-
tial thoughts. He remembered how a friend of his had
been involved in a mid-air collision and had para-
chuted to safety, but a few days later the RAF Equipment Officer had come along to him with enormous
books and carbon papers galore, to tell him that he
owed the RAF 2s. 6d. for not bringing the release-
handle back with his parachute. So, to spite any offici-
ous equipment officer who might challenge him at some
later date, Tom Gleave remembers deliberately throw-
ing the release-handle away as he floated down to
earth.

When he landed Tom Gleave was given a lift into
Orpington in a car, then wheeled into hospital in a
barrow! He remembers his skin and tissue blowing up
'like a Michelin Man' and the onset of pain. He remembers waking up under bright lights and asking a nurse:
'How long will I be here, six weeks?' And the nurse had
replied, 'Oh yes, something like that.' It was eleven and a
half months before he could fly again.

While his face was badly damaged by those few seconds
in the burning aircraft, yet more damage was caused by
the treatment which he received for those burns. He
received the tannic acid treatment, which was the best
then available. As a result of the acid drawing his skin
together he lost his eyelids and his nose. When he was
eventually moved to East Grinstead he was able to enjoy
the new saline bath treatment. He enjoyed it so much that

he would lie in the bath for long periods of time even taking a book with him.

Tom Gleave remembers his first meeting with McIndoe. The famous surgeon came into the Ward one evening wearing a multi-coloured dressing gown and a green hat. He had been operating all day but found time to sit at the end of the bed of his new patient and start chatting. In a few minutes, Tom Gleave forgot that he was talking to the 'Maestro'. They were chatting so easily 'I might have been conversing with the next door neighbour about his new cabbages. There was no question of one being the patient and the other the surgeon. We were just two people who had met in the ward.'

It was McIndoe's great gift that he was able to put people at their ease so quickly. When he discussed treatment it was not a matter of him telling his patient what he was about to do, it seemed to the patient that he was being asked his advice. He said to Tom Gleave, 'You know you'll be much better with a decent nose, you ought to have one.' Tom Gleave said, 'Okay', and in time he had a new nose.

For a while, as his treatment progressed, Tom Gleave remained unsightly. His head was shaved and he needed a pedicle to transfer new skin from his forehead to the damaged area, his nose. He had a plastic nostril, and indeed still wears this at night. 'Once, at a dance, it fell out. I stopped the band playing and said "I've lost my nose." Everybody started searching around – and, just as we spotted it someone trod on it.'

How did Tom Gleave cope with disfigurement? Most importantly he had a good marriage. And, as he sits in his riverside room, beside a cabinet containing mementos and souvenirs, talking with his wife Beryl, you know instinctively the value of that support.

The next most important thing, to him, was that every part of him was in working order. It was important to have eyelids that blinked and a nose through which he could breathe. Above all he wanted to go back to flying. The cosmetic treatment could come later. When he went home

to his wife and son in Chichester, people would stare at
him, but he shrugged it off. He had complete confidence
in McIndoe and knew that in the end a more normal face
would emerge from the surgeon's work. Sometimes when
people stared Tom Gleave felt like saying, 'Go on then,
have a bloody good look. Stare. But I shan't always be like
this. . . . '

The long-term damage which can be inflicted on the
spirit of an individual depends on two things: the nature
of the injury, obviously, but also the individual's ambitions. A man aspiring to be a great pianist who loses a
hand or even a finger, or a man who hopes to become a
great actor and whose face becomes damaged, can perhaps feel the effect of a smaller injury more acutely than
a less single-minded individual suffering greater disabilities.

What is it that enables a man to get through the trauma
of injury and come to terms with the barbs of life that
follow? It is the view of the Chief Guinea Pig that 'sheer
guts' gets you through. But there is one proviso. There are
some people who are, by nature, braver than others and 'it
would be wrong to criticise anybody not knowing what
they have to contend with inside themselves.'

Gleave, another man who's observed bravery and
cowardice at close quarters, supplements Russell Davies's
thoughts on the subject. Gleave is a large, warm, comfortable person. His words contain no hint of censure.

'You see, some people have got it and others haven't.
Now take our blind boys, for instance. They're full of guts.
They're incredible. You've met them, haven't you?
They've obviously got more than their fair share of guts.
They were at the front of the queue when courage was
handed out.'

Does that imply a fear inside himself of being blinded?
He pauses. 'I don't know how I'd have coped with that. I
can imagine myself compensating for a lot of things. But
blindness – I just don't know. Yet they've learned to live
with it most successfully. I'm not saying it hasn't hurt, and
hurt like hell. But they've done it. That's why I'm damn

sure they'll never want for anything. Not as long as I'm alive.'

Not as long as the Club is in existence? 'Yes, I'm sure that's true as well. But, looking ahead, we've a real problem just around the corner. A number of the boys are losing their sight as they get older. It was already impaired, and now it's disappearing. How are they going to cope with this fresh crisis?' Gleave worries about this as he sees the Club continuing McIndoe's work and enabling every Guinea Pig to be a worthwhile member of the community. McIndoe was determined that no Guinea Pig would go into an institution and Tom Gleave is just as determined. 'We don't care a damn what it costs,' he says.

There are two sides to the Guinea Pig Club. There is the comradeship of the Guinea Pigs themselves, and the work done behind the scenes by Blackie, Russell Davies, Bernard Arch, Connie McIndoe and the others. Tom Gleave, uniquely, sees both sides of the Club's activities from within. He is a Guinea Pig, in that he has qualified through his injuries. But he is also one of the officials, dealing with the Club's business activities, helping individual Guinea Pigs, fighting battles with departments where necessary, and always dealing with a mounting pile of paper work. He is very much the Pig in the middle . . . .

It is interesting to watch the way he resists the temptation of living in the past. It is true he has his mementos of the Battle of Britain. Through meticulous research, he was even able to locate the spot at Knockholt in Kent where his aeroplane crashed and he has salvaged a piece of the aircraft as a souvenir. But he keeps up to date in two ways. He lectures to varied audiences, showing them the machines he fought in. Many of the schoolboys are only a few months younger than the recruits who came to his squadron in the desperate days of 1940. In addition, as Chief Guinea Pig, he lives with the problems which the victims of the war still face today. At any moment, as he is ferreting through the archives for a new piece for his historical jigsaw, his telephone can ring and he can find himself catapulted into the present, his advice urgently required to aid a Guinea Pig in need. And when the call to 'scramble' comes, Tom Gleave, the administrator, moves as quickly as ever he did as a Battle of Britain pilot. . . .

4

Geoffrey Page

Of all the Guinea Pigs, Geoffrey Page was probably McIndoe's favourite. The views of the early members of the Club are quite clear on the subject: 'They were like father and son ... if ever there was a party, and some of the Guinea Pigs had to be taken home, Geoffrey always helped The Boss, and it was McIndoe who would run Geoffrey back to the hospital. ... The Boss had a special relationship with all the Guinea Pigs. But, with Geoffrey, it seemed very special . . . . '

'Father and son'. More accurately, they behaved like brothers, elder and younger. Page, debonair, determined, witty, was there in East Grinstead almost from the beginning of everything, because he was one of the early casualties of the Battle of Britain; there as the Club grew, as the struggles with authority to establish the rights of these sorely injured men were won; there once more in 1942 when he was shot down again and returned to the healing hands of McIndoe.

Like so many other Guinea Pigs, flying has been the great passion in Geoffrey Page's life, even from the age of five, when a photograph was taken of the young Geoffrey building an aircraft carrier out of wood. 'As long as I can remember, I've always wanted to be a pilot.'

So, in 1937, he joined the London University Air Squadron. He was seventeen and studying aeronautical engineering at Imperial College. By the time war was declared Page, and the other university pilots, were 80 or 90 per cent trained. They were some of the earliest members of 'The Few'. He became a Guinea Pig one hot

Geoffrey Page

August day in 1940. Ten British planes took off to defend
Manston Airfield in Kent. Ninety German aircraft, Dor-
nier bombers and escorting Messerschmitt fighters, were
over the Thames estuary when they were intercepted by
the Hurricanes. Climbing to attack, the British aircraft
were vulnerable. They were caught in cross-fire from the
Dorniers' rear guns. Then, the German fighters dived on
them. Page remembers 'things like electric light bulbs
flashing past me. Suddenly, there was a great explosion.
The smaller fuel tank, the only one of the three tanks
which was not self-sealing, was hit. It was positioned
almost in the lap of the pilot.

I was in the middle of a blazing inferno. The whole
episode is instantly memorable. It was a cross-roads
in my life. It was like one of those war combat films
where an aeroplane is flying along and then, suddenly, there's a whoosh and there is a blazing bombshell
in the sky. When you find yourself sitting in the
middle of this, I suppose the beautiful thing about it
is that your basic RAF training stands you in good
stead.

Initially you record absolute terror. There's no
question about that at all; I'm not ashamed to say it.
You're screaming with fear. Secondly, the thing is
happening so quickly, if you don't get out within a
few seconds, you're dead. You can see your hands
burning in front of you. The life is just going out of
you.

They say the temperature goes from 5° to 350°
Centigrade – which is fairly hot, like a cooking oven
– in about seven seconds. It's as if someone was
putting an enormous blow torch on you. But the
RAF training gives you a life-saving drill which you
do instinctively. You pull the split-pin out of the
sub-harness, disentangle your oxygen and radio
communication and roll the aeroplane. It takes just a
few seconds but you do it as if it were second nature.
And, after that, you're tumbling head over heels

through the air. You start to fumble with the rip cord of your parachute but my hands were badly burned and I couldn't pull the rip cord. Yet the instinct for survival is enormous – so, despite the pain, the rip-cord was pulled. . . .

Geoffrey Page had his first saline bath where the Thames Estuary meets the North Sea. He was taken to Margate Hospital and, later, to the Royal Masonic Hospital in Hammersmith, where McIndoe found him.

Page was lying in the Royal Masonic Hospital, Hammersmith, London when the ward sister asked him whether he was able to receive a visitor. When he said that he was, she left the ward, but left a file of papers on the cradle over his legs. Geoffrey Page's curiosity got the better of him and he eased his way forward. In his injured condition, face and hands cruelly burned, it took him about fifteen minutes but, eventually, he got the file between his elbows, turned it over to see what the medical assessment of his condition might be. All the file said was: 'Air Ministry permission is hereby granted for Mr Archibald Hector McIndoe, to visit one patient, Geoffrey Page, Royal Masonic Hospital.'

The following day in came this man who looked like a young Harold Lloyd, squat, wearing spectacles. He was a delightful person and he sat on my bed and asked me various questions. I did not know that he was a doctor. He asked nothing medical at all. He wanted to know the type of aircraft I was flying, whether I had been wearing goggles and practical things like that. He said, 'Were you wearing gloves?' I'll always remember his answer. I said, 'No.' He said, 'clot.' I certainly had been a clot, gloves would have saved my hands. Then he said, 'I'll be seeing you again.' And he did, at East Grinstead.

The realisation that he was going to be badly disfigured came only slowly to Page. When he was first in hospital, he imagined getting back to his squadron 'within a week'. When things took longer than a week, the people at East Grinstead would reassure him, saying 'Don't worry, you'll be there soon.' 'Soon' was to be two years away, two years in hospital, during which he was kept going by two things: what he describes as his 'stupid mania to get back to flying,' and his hatred for the Germans. 'I made a resolution that, for every operation I had, I would shoot down one German aeroplane when I got back to flying. After all, those operations weren't too much fun, you know.'

He had fifteen operations in two years. Then he went back to operational flying. He shot down seventeen enemy aircraft.

Understandably, part of his bitterness was caused by his disfiguring injuries, for he had never anticipated being injured. Is it not the beauty of youth, Geoffrey Page wonders, that youth believes itself immortal? It is a double-edged weapon, of course. It brings both confidence and over-confidence, which is why eager youngsters drive their cars at high speeds. 'We just happened to fly aeroplanes at high speed – and someone gave us a medal instead of burying us in graveyards for driving cars too quickly. . . . ' Page learned that he couldn't live on hate. When he flew again, he was sustained by a cold determination to shoot down as many Germans as he could. He became more and more experienced and got his own fighter wing. Then the lust for revenge burnt itself out. 'I found myself not liking myself. I was full of hate, and it was damaging me. I felt myself drained of energy. Mind you, I was exhausted by my operational flying – but how long can you carry on a vendetta?'

At the airborne attack on Arnhem, Page was shot down again. It was a very different Geoffrey Page who returned to East Grinstead for further treatment. One of only two Guinea Pigs to qualify twice, the other being Frankie Truhlar, who was later to be killed in a flying accident after the war.

Page found the hospital a bigger and perhaps more

institutionalised place, institutionalised in the sense that Guinea Piggery was now accepted as part of the treatment, and officially encouraged. What had been experimental was now routine.

Page had always kept in touch with McIndoe and the hospital. During his leaves, he'd stayed with the surgeon. Relationships were close. They shared an affection for McIndoe's indispensable theatre sister, Jill Mullins.

Many Guinea Pigs, on a foundation of gratitude, put McIndoe on a pedestal of perfection. To Page, he was:

A normal human being with a great insight into human frailties. He was capable of what, to Air Force officials, must have seemed inexcusable skulduggery. The regulations of the day stated that, if a member of air crew was off active duty for more than eighteen months, he was automatically invalided out of the service. If any of his patients had ambitions to return to flying, and because of their operations were going to be out of action for eighteen months or more, McIndoe would pull every string he could to find the man a job. Usually a fake job, too. So that, theoretically, the pilot had gone back to work, but he was probably sitting with his feet up in a pub, doing nothing at all, waiting for the next operation. Provided you had three months working at your hypothetical job, you were then free for another eighteen months before the regulations began to apply again.

Geoffrey Page managed to be away for two years before going back to flying. When he did return to flying it took a while to adjust. His hands were tender. And he had memories. . . . His first fifty hours of flying were non-operational. He went to an air training calibration unit and spent many tedious hours flying up and down 'getting bored to tears'. But it gave him the feel of flying again. He had some doubts as to whether he would be able to cope with bad weather again but, before long, he got back into the rhythm of it all. 'It was like riding a bike – you don't forget.'

Did he fear that he might be shot down again? 'It never entirely left me. But I coped with it, being a little older and a little wiser.'

As the war came to an end, Geoffrey Page went on a tour of the United States, talking of his experiences as a Guinea Pig. There, he met the English actor, Nigel Bruce. 'One day', he said to me, 'you must come back when the war's finished and marry our daughter, who's in the Canadian Air Force.' Geoffrey Page returned to Britain, and began working as a test pilot with Vickers Armstrong. He wrote to Nigel Bruce's daughter whom he'd never met and said, 'Behave yourself or I'll come back and marry you one day.' He did go back. They got married. McIndoe became godfather to one of their children.

Today, Geoffrey Page is a successful businessman in Switzerland. He is not a man who has been badly disfigured in the long-term. His scars are obvious only if you are looking for them. His 'enemies' he says are little children who see him on a bus or in a railway carriage and spot the scars within five seconds. Suddenly, everyone will hear a little voice piping up, 'Mummy, look at him.' Then he is conscious of all eyes on the bus or in the carriage looking at him even if they themselves had not noticed anything at all before.

These days Geoffrey Page prefers to travel by car. However much he was prepared for disfigurement by the Ward Three rehabilitation, what Tom Gleave describes as 'the barbs of the outside world' can still hurt.

Bill Simpson

5

Bill Simpson

The first thing to notice on meeting Bill Simpson is that he smokes. Not a cigar nor even cigarettes, though that would be difficult enough for a man whose hands are no more than stumps. He smokes a pipe. He has all the usual pipe smoker's quirks. He puffs at his pipe in short spells. He plays with it and battles constantly to keep it alight. It is typical of Bill Simpson that, even in the small things, he cannot resist a challenge.

Bill Simpson became a Guinea Pig on 10 May 1940. He was flying a Battle bomber at low level attacking a column of German troops coming into Luxembourg. During the attack, the plane was hit and, with flames streaming from the engine, he just managed to land in a green field somewhere in the Belgian Ardennes. He was pulled out of the burning cockpit in the nick of time by the air gunner and observer. They dragged him to the ground and rolled him in the long grass. Then they carried him to safety fifty yards away from the burning aeroplane.

He knew from the first moment that he was badly burned. He stood apart and watched what was happening to his other self. He was surprised at what he saw. His hands were not red or bleeding; they were like skeletons, transfixed. The whole of his body felt frozen together. It was only after an hour or so that he began to feel pain.

When everything started to happen, Bill Simpson felt that he would die. It had seemed such a long time before anybody had come to his aid. He was surprised when his two colleagues had come to pull him out of the inferno.

If the moments in the blazing cockpit had seemed an

55

age, the next eighteen months were an eternity. For the first ten of those months, Bill Simpson lay helpless, near death, being moved from one French hospital to another to keep him away from Hitler's advancing army. He was treated for burns in the unsophisticated manner of the day. To make matters worse, there were often shortages of medical dressings and day after day, he was in acute pain. He was quite helpless and he was frequently moved under unpleasant, uncomfortable and rather frightening circumstances. He was, mentally, at a very low ebb. He could see no sign of hope, particularly as he watched France collapsing around him. 'I never wished for death. But there were certainly times when I did not want to live,' he says.

By October 1941, Bill Simpson had recovered sufficiently to be repatriated to England. From Vichy France, he came home via Spain and Portugal. He was in a terrible mess. He weighed about seven stone, compared with his present twelve stone. He was scarred, he had no eyelids and the whole of his face was badly burned. His hands were bandaged and virtually useless. His legs had barely recovered from the year he had spent in bed. They were stiff and burned and one knee would not bend. He also had a burned foot. He could not feed himself. In short, he was entirely dependent on other people. Bill Simpson felt he had lost everything worthwhile.

His homecoming was not happy. He was angry. He remembered what had happened to him and saw what was happening in Britain, all around him. He felt himself a spectator of an unbelievably tragic scene. After his experiences in France, he felt that Britain, too, was collapsing. And yet he felt that nobody in England had any concept of what was happening on the Continent. Nor did they care. Nor did they heed the warning signals. He seethed with frustrated fury that nobody seemed aware of the tragedy that he thought was coming.

In addition to these feelings, Simpson discovered he was edgy about people when they wanted to help him – particularly if they wanted to do things for him which he felt he could do perfectly well himself. It's a feeling not unknown to anyone who is handicapped.

Perhaps the hardest part of all was coming home to his family. Bill Simpson's wife was shattered on seeing her husband. She could not conceive what had happened to him. If she had had any idea of what war injuries were, she visualised a gallant wounded soldier with his arm in a sling, no blood, no smell of rotting flesh. For his first wife had a horror of blood. Later on in the war, she was to go with the American Red Cross to the Normandy landings. Then she understood, but it was a hard way to learn, and, by that time, it was too late. Bill Simpson's first marriage was over.

For a number of months before his return to England, Bill Simpson had had a premonition that his marriage would not survive. Perhaps he was aware that his experience was changing him. Talk to him today and he feels that, before the war, he'd been a difficult person to live with because he had been young, immature and ambitious in a narrow all-consuming sense. In the two years apart from his wife, he had grown up. Away from each other, they had had different experiences and so by the time of Bill Simpson's return, they were both different people.

The extent of the burns, Bill believes, triggered the break-up. Yet he also believes the break-up may well have happened anyway.

And what of his own family? Simpson's mother took her son's injuries very stoically. She was ill and he delayed seeing her until he had had some plastic surgery, 'to tidy myself up', because he feared the shock of seeing him might make her worse.

Bill Simpson was one of the first patients at East Grinstead's Ward Three. Sir Archibald McIndoe's 'tidying up' process began by giving Simpson new eyelids. Slowly but surely, the face was reconstructed and the hands repaired as much as possible. With determination and some ingenuity, Simpson learnt how to use his re-formed stumps to be able to write, eat, hold a telephone and even,

the ultimate achievement at the time, use a telephone and
write at the same time.

To Simpson, the atmosphere at East Grinstead in the
Guinea Pig ward, was very highly charged, 'sexually,
socially, emotionally and in every way you can think'.
Ward Three had an atmosphere of deep friendship, he
recollects, as a result of a shared experience between
fellow Guinea Pigs and between the patients and medical
staff. The experience was of pain and shock. But the
atmosphere was one of hope, engendered by nurses and
by doctors and by the fellow patients.

The ward, however, was a very noisy place, something
which did not always endear itself to Simpson. Even now
he describes himself as 'unclubbable', and attending the
reunion weekend takes an effort, however much he enjoys
meeting old friends. In a way he remembers he felt
slightly detached from the ward. He was, after all, a few
years older than many of his fellow patients. But he was at
one with the other Guinea Pigs in viewing McIndoe as a
great man, a man whom he respected enormously. Simpson saw him as a man of tremendous optimism, tremendous vitality, a man who laughed a lot and lived a lot.
McIndoe himself performed most of the operations on
Simpson.

There were, it is fair to note, one or two Guinea Pigs
who didn't love McIndoe as much as the others. He was
for instance capable of carrying out surgical practical
jokes, and would do so if he thought it taught a patient a
lesson. Simpson remembers one or two people who had
operations which seemed more complicated than some
surgeons might have thought necessary. There was one
Guinea Pig who had rather a lot to say about delays to his
operations. When it was his turn to 'go on the slab', more
happened to him than he had expected. Some of Sir
Archibald's jokes were rough.

The nurses in the ward identified closely with the
Guinea Pigs and the task of rehabilitation. If Simpson was
going to marry again, it was perhaps inevitable that it
should be to one of his nurses.

He remembers reservations about going into a second marriage. Would he make a mess of marriage again? He had a feeling that the marriage would not work out and yet he went ahead with it. Looking back, without apportioning blame, he thinks that he and his second wife were in fact unsuited. There were many people who told them so before they married. But they were both stubborn, and, he reflects, the marriage brought happiness and it brought children and, even after divorce, friendship.

By the time Bill Simpson's second marriage was dissolved, he was well on the way with his post-war career. He had become a journalist and later became a public relations consultant. Again it is typical of Simpson, that he chose a job which, on the surface, would appear to be particularly difficult for a man handicapped with no hands and a damaged face. Looking back on the days of the break-up of his second marriage, Bill Simpson describes himself as having been 'bloody difficult'. He was trying far too hard to come to terms with the tests of life. 'I was very selfish and very self-centred and determined to burst through every kind of barrier and, without quite knowing what I wanted to do, I was determined to do it.' He had started life a fairly determined fellow. After what he had been through, he was determined to the point of obsession. He did not want to prove anything in particular; he did things, he recalls, 'because they were difficult to do.'

Was Bill Simpson seeking to prove that he was as good as the next man, despite his handicap? It is not as easy as that. Simpson admits that life is frequently difficult. There are things about being disabled and burned which are very unpleasant. The colour of burns is unpleasant. When operations go wrong, smell is unpleasant. Movement is ungainly. It is difficult for many Guinea Pigs to go into a restaurant and eat in public, so eating becomes a challenge. But because so many things are difficult for Bill Simpson, difficult because he has to work everything out for himself, he has tended to develop into a person who does a little bit extra all round, all the time. In a way, it has become a drug to keep on doing things which are theoretically impossible. A man's aim must exceed his grasp or what is a heaven for?

Bill Simpson has achieved much in life. He became top man in British European Airways in his chosen field, that of public relations. Yet still he doesn't feel that he has succeeded. He feels today that he has 'free-wheeled' in a non-creative job. He believes he ought to have started some other job when he found things getting easier. If you like, when he began to succeed.

He was attracted to journalism by the challenge of going out and facing the world rather than sitting back and being helped. Now, however, he feels that he has been something of a spectator. In his job, he is an intermediary, helping or hindering other people in what they do. If he had his time again, he reflects, he would rather have built a bridge – even if he had had to do it with his own hands. Rather than reporting the achievement of others, he should have created something.

And the fact of being a Guinea Pig poses one, unanswerable question. Does one achieve because one is a Guinea Pig receiving special favours, or does one achieve despite one's handicap? Though Simpson has been successful, it would be misleading to pretend he hasn't experienced disappointment: the moments throughout his life when he has sought jobs and missed them; the moments when, as a public relations man, he has sought to influence, and failed.

Is it a consideration that's always hovering in the background? 'Yes.' Whatever the situation, be it in business or social life or whatever the human relationship?

'Yes, definitely. Not that it's an obsession. It's simply . . . well, it's often there.'

Simpson knows he is too flamboyant for some people. He knows some don't like his style. But does his disfigurement influence decisions in any way? No one can provide the answer for Simpson. Sometimes he thinks that it is a silly and unworthy thought and he dismisses it, only to find his mind comes back to it. 'The trick', says

Simpson, 'is to function in an untroubled environment where the answer to the question doesn't matter so much anymore.'

It is in his third marriage that he has found that. He married for the third time fourteen years ago. He describes it as a happy marriage. But it is a marriage in which both partners have to work hard because both have been married before.

One unusual thing about it is that Bill Simpson's wife is an Orthodox Jew and he remains a Christian. It is through her Jewish background that Bill Simpson has learnt a tolerance which he did not have before. He has learnt racial tolerance, tolerance of religion and tolerance of human nature, a marked contrast to the Bill Simpson of the war years. Today, he acknowledges that the Jewishness of his wife has enabled him to understand his position as a Guinea Pig with more sensitivity. A Jew, he explains, is a member of a minority which faces castigation, isolation, sometimes danger. Being a Guinea Pig also makes one a member of a minority – not a dangerous one but a difficult one. It is a tough experience to be in a minority. You are different and people do not like people to be different. They are wary of people who are Guinea Pigs and often they are wary of people who are Jews. They don't like them to be Catholics, if they themselves are Protestants. If they are Catholics, they don't like them to be Protestants. To be different is to be viewed with misgivings. It goes back, Bill Simpson continues, right back to early childhood when every child at school wants to wear a uniform. The pressure is to look exactly the same.

Gaining tolerance means to Bill Simpson not only accepting that people have the right to feel and think and act differently, but even liking to think that. People have a right to be different.

In some very practical ways, Christianity and Judaism meet head on in Bill Simpson's house. Friday night, the Sabbath night is a very special occasion with prayers and a special meal.

'Even very un-family people will come home for that. Each faith supplements the other, you know. The beauty and pathos of the Christian service, the music and softness. Clarity and the realisation that you're an individual and that there may be nothing beyond – I think that's what I get out of the Jewish religion.'

In the war years, Bill Simpson says, he was too much of a sinner to be a true Christian. He had a feeling for Christianity but he did not believe in everything that the Christian creed sets out. He was religious, he says, in that he wanted to believe. But as war ground on, he became disillusioned. He became more intellectual in his approach to life, he became more questioning. He ceased to have a blind faith. Now, he has a faith that there is some purpose to life and likes to feel that that purpose is a good rather than a bad purpose.

Life as a Guinea Pig has taught Bill Simpson humility, smallness. When he first flew, and particularly when he first flew alone, the ground disappeared beneath him and the people and the houses became just microscopic dots. He was a young man then, energetic and ambitious. He felt, he says, a very small speck in a vast something. Today, Bill Simpson sees himself again as a tiny speck – but very much part of the order of things.

6

Bertram Owen Smith

The man in green crouches over the operating table. His hands are short and square and quick. The surgeon's mask covers only his mouth, leaving his nose free, because that's the way he prefers it. The face bears the savage scars of war, for Bertram Owen Smith is a Guinea Pig.

The harsh white light concentrates on a black hand that Owen Smith is reconstructing. For this is Salisbury, Rhodesia, and, if he ever pauses to reflect on the situation, life for Owen Smith has come full circle. Nearly forty years after he was himself shattered by injury, he operates on the victims of the conflict between black and black, and white and black, as Rhodesia becomes Zimbabwe. He is a plastic surgeon, just as McIndoe was before him. He fights to restore others, just as McIndoe used his skill to restore him.

> We spend at least a third of all our time in the operating theatre working on war casualties. You don't see so many burns as there were at East Grinstead. After all, it's less of an aerial war than it was in 1940 and, in any case, they've learned a little about aircraft design. You're no longer sitting on the fuel tank, I guess!
>
> But the injuries caused by the missiles are devastating. And there are the usual refinements of war, such as land-mines and bullets and shrapnel and rocket fragments, all of which keep us busy.

Owen Smith lives in a lush suburb of Salisbury, amid the

Bertram Owen Smith

swimming pools and tennis clubs. He is philosophical about the transition to majority rule, though he joined the fight to prevent it. For a while he was an MP, a member of former Premier Ian Smith's Rhodesia Front Party. He didn't relish the experience. 'Politics weren't for me. But, after UDI [Ian Smith's declaration of independence from Britain] I felt Harold Wilson had sold us down the river and I wanted to do what I could to help my country through what I knew was going to be a difficult period.'

Owen Smith is softly spoken. There is hardly a trace of the accent of South Wales, where he was born. He is not self-conscious about using words like 'patriotism' for, as he says, 'I fought for my country in 1940 and, right or wrong, I feel my cause over the past few years was equally just . . . . '

He volunteered for that first battle, the Battle of Britain. He was seventeen and he wanted to join the Fleet Air Arm. They wouldn't have him because he was too young, so he went next door 'to the RAF and they were only too pleased to have me . . . . '

It was a time when Britain was desperately short of aircrew. Machines they could find and build, though that was difficult enough, but men had to be trained and that took time. Only the fact that many British aircrew baled out or crash-landed, in Britain, and could thus return to the fight, kept the RAF in the air. Many Guinea Pigs returned to flying duties, even between operations, as Owen Smith was to do after he was badly burned.

Blackie remembers the young Owen Smith during his months at East Grinstead as he waited for one of the twenty-six operations on his face or hands. Owen Smith was eighteen years old.

He'd worked in an insurance office while he waited to start his flying training, and I remember him as someone who seemed desperately young. Our job, as it was with all of them, was to motivate them into overcoming the shock to their system and their pride. And while he lay there in bed, week after week,

Owen Smith began to show an amazing interest in
the complexities of the surgery itself that was going
to be used to save his face. He wanted to know about
the techniques. He talked to anyone and everyone
about it. And he let it be known that he wanted to
become a doctor.

Now, there seemed no way that he would achieve
this. He was a young lad who, as far as I know,
hadn't even got his school certificate [the school-
leaving examination]. We talked about him and his
ambitions and we just didn't *think* he'd ever achieve
what he wanted to do, we *knew* he wouldn't achieve
it. But we supplied him with the books and encouraged him in his studies. Because, from our point of
view, at that time, the important thing was that he
wanted to achieve. He wanted to help himself. If he
failed, well, that was something to cope with later on.

It is a matter of record that Bertram Owen Smith proved
wrong those who had doubted him. He matriculated, he
qualified as a doctor and became a Fellow of the Royal
College of Surgeons. He was at the Royal Marsden
Hospital in London, working mainly on what he describes
as repairs 'following major surgery on malignancies' when
he suggested that many of the techniques he'd seen
McIndoe employ at the Queen Victoria Hospital might
profitably be used in his current speciality. The hospital
agreed and Owen Smith returned to East Grinstead, this
time as a surgeon. Owen Smith recalls:

After a few months, the Boss very kindly said: 'Why
don't you take up plastic surgery, become a special-
ist? I think you have a bent for it. I think it's the work
you'll enjoy doing for the rest of your life as a
surgeon.' And I agreed. So I became a senior
registrar at Queen Victoria Hospital and, from him,
learned the business from top to bottom. It was a
tremendous privilege.

Many of the Guinea Pigs had a close relationship with McIndoe like Page, Gleave and Hillary, but Owen Smith's relationship differed from all the others in one respect. Certainly, there was the gratitude that all the Guinea Pigs felt and feel. After all, he owed McIndoe his face. But there was more, the feeling a pupil has for his master. He is still deferential about McIndoe:

> I don't think one ever had the presumption to think that one would emulate the Boss; it was enough to try to follow his example ... you couldn't give up on anything not with a chap like the Boss; it was a matter of pride that you didn't let him down. I've never, truly never, met a man like him; he didn't tolerate fools gladly, nor incompetence, but I'll never forget the patience he showed me in those early days, when I became almost a permanent resident of the operating theatre, watching how he worked, asking him all the questions, trying to understand his explanations. Whether he believed I'd ever become a surgeon, I'll never know.

He acknowledges that his experience as a Guinea Pig have given him a privileged insight into the feelings of those who now come to him for help. He knows about pain and shock and despair and the rekindling of hope. He remembers it all vividly. He was the pilot of a Whitley bomber, the plane nicknamed, with more than a trace of bitterness, the Flying Coffin. They were two-engined aircraft, and if one engine failed, particularly when the plane was fully loaded with high explosive or incendiary bombs, there was precious little anyone could do to keep the Whitley in the air, which is precisely what happened one dark night in 1941. Owen Smith remembers:

> The engines coughed and spluttered as we were half way along our take-off run, but they picked up again. I had to make a quick decision; whether to stop or go on. The engines sounded all right so I decided to

press on. We got off the ground, but as we reached
around three hundred feet, one of the engines
packed up altogether. Which was a worry. It was
pitch black out there. We'd left the aerodrome
behind and all I could do was sit there, and keep her
steady and hope she came down somewhere where
we had a chance of getting away with it.

Owen Smith and his crew were lucky. They came down in
a short meadow, only two hundred yards long. But they
flew in over a river and the undercarriage wheel struck the
river bank, slowed the aircraft's flight and enabled Owen
Smith to pull up just before he ran out of open land. The
aircraft stopped just short of a copse of trees. If the
Whitley had run into the wood, nothing would have
prevented the plane, with its full load of fuel and high
explosives, being totally destroyed. But Owen Smith knew
none of this. He knew only that he was down in one piece.
He knew also that his starboard engine was on fire and
that he was being burned. The way out of the plane was
through a side window in the cockpit. The window was
jammed. There were three men inside the burning plane,
the fourth, the rear gunner, had stepped out unscathed.

We kicked at the window. We hammered at it and
eventually got it open. The three of us squeezed out,
myself, the second pilot and the wireless operator. I
was aware of the fact that I was in flames but I didn't
feel any pain. Thank God I was still wearing my
flying gloves.
    I only knew we'd been in that aircraft longer than
we'd wanted to be. And I also knew that there was an
awful lot of explosion still to come. So we just ran.
And, fortunately, we ran in the right direction. Past
the tail of the aircraft and straight into the river.
Which not only put out the flames but, because we
were now standing on the river bed behind the river
bank, protected us when the Whitley went up. And
how it went up.

You know, it's amazing what the body will stand. I know it was dark but I can honestly say that I didn't realise I was badly burned. When the bangs and pops finished, we staggered out of the shallow river and made our way across the field and people came to meet us as they heard us chattering and stumbling away. And only then did I begin to feel a bit of pain. So I said, and I remember this, 'Please could you take us to the nearest doctor,' very politely. And they did. And a very unhappy village medico, who obviously saw how seriously we were burned, had to cope with us.

I remember sitting around his kitchen table, while his wife made us all a cup of tea, and he dissolved little morphia tablets in a teaspoon over a spirit lamp, so that he could try to help us with our pain. He gave us the morphia, and, to be truthful, I don't remember much about the next few days.

Nor did his crew, co-pilot Freddie Whitehorn, and Canadian wireless operator Gerry Dufort, both of whom also became Guinea Pigs.

Owen Smith knew despair in those early months. He knew it and he recognised it.

There were some men at the hospital who just couldn't cope with the whole business. They just seemed emotionally incapable of coming to terms with it, everything that had happened to them in such a short space of time. The ones who'd say very little and, psychologically, would go away and hide in a corner. I felt sorry for them, and I'm glad to say that, among the Guinea Pigs, they were in a minority. But they helped me to be even more determined not to give in.

And, as he tends his patients today, he remembers this.

It's what goes on inside a man's head that matters,

more than anything else. I know this from being disabled myself, as much as anything I have observed in others. It doesn't matter whether it's a social disablement, like my disfigurement, or a physical, functional disablement, like the loss of a limb.

Very early on, while he's still grieving over what's happened to him, he's got to make a decision. Is he going to make the best of things, in other words, is he going to utilise to the full what remains? Or is he going to go through the rest of his life bemoaning what has happened to him, becoming a burden to himself and to all whom he meets?

Now, no one pretends this is an easy decision. But I believe that disabled people can be divided into these two clearly defined groups – those who try to achieve their maximum potential and those who go into a corner to weep with self-pity for the rest of their lives.

You have to make it. It does you good. It makes you look at yourself pretty clearly. You like some of the things you see, and you're not too keen on some of the other aspects of your own character. But the self-assessment involved in making the decision is bound to be of benefit.

Provided you make the right decision, that is . . . .

But some decisions are forced upon us by circumstances. Would Owen Smith, the young insurance clerk from South Wales, have become a plastic surgeon without the disasters of 1941? Could he have done so, without the injuries and disfigurement that led him to East Grinstead and Archibald McIndoe? Owen Smith says that to speculate isn't necessarily profitable but he believes, 'I wouldn't have achieved half of it without the experience, and the support I received at East Grinstead. I've been very lucky . . . .'

Of course, there are those who believe that a man largely makes his own luck.

7

George Bennions

Yorkshireman George 'Ben' Bennions is one of those rare
people who can claim that as a school boy, he was able to
announce what he wished to do in life – and then
proceeded to do it. Young Ben Bennions wanted to be
either a school master or to join the Air Force. In fact he
joined the Air Force and subsequently became a school
master. Significantly, once he had become a pilot, there
was no longer any alternative worth considering, because
Ben Bennions has conducted a fifty-year love affair with
flying.

It began when he joined up as an aircraft apprentice. He
was a lad of ambition and was recommended for cadet-
ship at Cranwell. He went there at the end of 1931. His
initial six-hours flying instruction in an Avro 504K
confirmed in his mind that he wanted to be a pilot and in
the collective mind of the RAF that they wanted him to
train as a pilot. Ben Bennions was aware of, but not
deterred by, the social distinctions which then existed
within the RAF. He was very much from a working-
class background. His contemporaries tended to have
come from public school. If anything, Ben Bennions
found the social differences a motivation. He felt that
he wanted to prove that he could do what he set out to
do.

At the outbreak of the Second World War, he was a
Sergeant Pilot, flying Spitfires. He remembers the first
occasion on which he flew a Spitfire, at the end of 1938.
He flew his Spitfire out of Catterick, not a very large
aerodrome, and had quite a problem taking off. This

George Bennions

model had a thick wooden-bladed air screw at the front and did not accelerate very quickly; the take-off run was much longer than it was for the later Spitfires.

'But once in the air the Spitfire was a lovely aeroplane, ladylike, smooth to handle and responding quickly.' Note it was, and still is, a love affair.

Bennions remembers the remark by a German pilot, when talking to Goering, that he needed 'a squadron of Spitfires' to win the war. But he also remembers occasions when he would have preferred a Messerschmitt 109. They could fly higher and dive faster. Despite the advantage, Ben Bennions shot down ten 109s from his Spitfire.

His first combat came on 28 July 1940, early in the morning, over Dover Castle. Bennions saw a 109 shooting at a friend of his. He watched his friend going down and was so angered that he could think only about revenge. He chased the 109 over to Calais and shot him down there. It was not until he was being shot at that he experienced fear.

Unless a man has a hide as thick as a horse, he must be frightened then. Ben Bennions remembers the feeling: the peculiar smell of burning metal when the bullets are striking home; the imagined smell of cordite, as the tracers snaked past. Bennions acknowledged that he might get shot down – but he was always confident that he would survive. Perhaps to be any good as a pilot in such circumstances you have to think that way.

During the long hot summer of 1940, he was shot down four times himself and crash landed once during a short period of only three months. He viewed each crash as just an accident. He never considered that each crash could possibly be his last. After all, it couldn't happen to him, could it? He thought he was too good for that. He was secure in his youthful vanity and he had the experience of at least five years' flying, unlike so many of the pilots, who were pitched into battle straight from training.

At that time, at the height of the Battle of Britain, Ben

Bennions and his colleagues were flying five or six missions a day. They would rise at half past four in the morning and finish, exhausted, at half past nine at night. Of all those hours, the most nerve-racking were not those in the air but those spent waiting on the ground, 'waiting and waiting and waiting for orders to take off for the next sortie', says Bennions.

As an older, more experienced pilot, Ben Bennions felt pity for some of the young men around him. They were keen but had little experience. Their chance of survival was not high. In particular, many of them had problems flying in the rarer air at high altitudes. Ben Bennions remembers one young man who, soon after joining the squadron, was shot down simply because he could not fly close enough to the main formation at 25,000 feet. As with many of the young volunteers, he had been taught to fly well at low altitudes, but most of the work during the Battle of Britain was being done at over 20,000 feet. Ben Bennions remembers feeling angry at the time. He felt that all too often the order to scramble was given too late and, as a result, he and his colleagues could only intercept the German formations from below. To attack out of the sun is to increase the chances of survival. His annoyance was directed mostly at the people who kept him sitting on the ground but, with hindsight, he acknowledges that he did not then realise the necessity of conserving the aircraft and of not having all aeroplanes in the air at the same time.

But what emotions did Ben Bennions feel towards the German pilots? For him, there was no hate against the person. He always felt sorry if the pilot did not bale out when he was shooting at a German fighter. But, when firing at the aircraft, he did not always remember that there was a person inside. He chose not to think about it, which was unlike one friend of his, a devout Roman Catholic, who, each time he shot an aeroplane down, was so upset by the experience that he would go to confess to the padre. In contrast, Ben Bennions saw his job as shooting aeroplanes down.

By October 1940 Ben Bennions had been operational for three months. It was felt he needed a rest. He agreed and had his pass prepared ready to go on leave. But he decided to have one more trip before he went.

He had been airborne for about an hour over the south coast of England patrolling up and down, getting short of oxygen flying at 25,000 feet when the squadron commander decided to head for home. Ben Bennions followed and began to lose height. On the way down he saw a squadron of Hurricanes with a large formation of German 109s about 5,000 feet above them. He called up the leader and, following the agreed system, he accelerated and flew ahead to indicate where the enemy aircraft were. The squadron leader looked ahead and saw only the Hurricanes. He called Ben Bennions back. They were Hurricanes not Messerschmitts. But Bennions carried on calling to the squadron leader that there were 109s above the Hurricanes. A moment later Bennions found himself alone with the 109s. There was no going back. He decided the easiest thing to do would be to get on the tail of the last 109 in the formation, shoot him down and get away.

But it didn't happen like that. A cannon shell exploded in the cockpit. The explosion damaged the left side of his face, his right arm and right leg. But most devastating of all it blinded him, taking away his left eye. He decided to bale out. He opened the side door, undid his oxygen with his left hand and rolled the aircraft over on to one side. He fell out of the plane, pulled his ripcord and then lost consciousness. The urge to escape is instinctive, but of his descent by parachute, Bennions remembers virtually nothing. He landed unconscious in a field to the north of Brighton and the next thing he remembers is a farmer speaking to him. Ben Bennions told him his name and asked that his squadron be informed. Then he passed out. He knew nothing more until he woke up several days later at East Grinstead.

For the first few days, on regaining consciousness, Ben

Bennions was completely blind. He could see only vaguely
the difference between light and dark. He was annoyed
with himself for having been so decisively shot down. He
was disappointed that his career was apparently at an end.
He was heartbroken at being unable to continue flying.
Despite being blinded permanently in one eye and badly
disfigured, his major concern was that he might be unable
to fly again. He resented being incapacitated and, looking
back, he thinks he must have been the most obstreperous
person in the hospital.

Of his early treatment, Ben Bennions remembers nothing. He was unconscious. He lost so much blood that he
needed five litres of plasma just to keep him alive. He
does remember, however, that when he began to regain
his sight, he was not allowed to look at himself in a mirror
for about a month.

As time passed and Ben Bennions grew fitter the urge to
fly again grew daily. While the Chief of the Air Staff
remained unwilling for a one-eyed incapacitated pilot to
take to the air again in a valuable RAF machine, Ben
Bennions had friends of a more generous nature. One
allowed him to fly his Spitfire, strictly unofficially. But
opportunities for unofficial flying were limited and so Ben
Bennions was recommended to the Central Flying School
for tests to see if his flying activities could be made official.
The school decided that he was fit to fly if he could pass a
medical test. The medical, however, was something of a
disappointment. Ben Bennions was given a category, A2B
Non-Operational. He had to have a passenger to look out
and he couldn't fly at night. In other words, he could fly
only on a fine day, with somebody else. Spitfires were
definitely out.

As a category, it was of little use to Ben Bennions. He
must do better than that. The opportunity came to go with
a squadron to North Africa. While he was there, he
was appointed Liaison Officer to the Americans, who
had just been equipped with Spitfires. He went with them
to an air base in Sicily. What happened next was inevitable, knowing Ben Bennions. Soon they were allowing

him to fly their aeroplanes whenever he wanted to. He went on convoy patrols but never flew in combat again.

When the war finished the RAF offered him a job in the Administrative and Special Duties Branch. Not surprisingly he turned the job down. You can't fly a desk. He decided to test that second alternative of long ago; he became a school teacher.

He threw himself into school teaching with great enthusiasm. He was keen on sport and specialised in physical education, mathematics and handicraft. But as he grew older and spent more time in the classroom, teaching became more burdensome. His mind was still on flying. Ben Bennions believes the lure of flying is nowhere better expressed than in *High Flight*, written by a young American pilot. Bennions knows it by heart.

Oh, I have slipped the surly bonds of earth,
and danced the skies on laughter, silvered wings,
sunward I've climbed, and joined the tumbling mirth
of sun-split clouds
and done a hundred things you have not dreamt of.
I've wheeled and soared and swung,
high in the sunlit sky, hovering there,
I've chased the shouting wind along
and flung my eager craft through footless hoards of air.
Up, up, the long, delirious burning blue,
I've topped the windswept heights,
where neither lark nor even eagle flew,
and whilst with high, uplifting mind, I've trod
the high untrespassed sanctity of space,
I've put out my hand and touched the face of God.

And Ben has written a verse of his own:

Through shades of blue and black and white,
I'll journey on to see the might
of outer space,

and there, in sanctity reposed my mind
encompassed, no-one knows what I may find.
Life's journey's end, eternal bliss
or just the everlasting kiss
– of death.

We were talking once, with Ben and his wife about an air
show, and Ben's availability to go there. 'He'll be there,'
she said. 'For Ben, everything takes second place to
flying.' And we all laughed because it was a joke. Partially.

Ben Bennions's return to flying involves an interesting
coincidence. During one dog fight with a German aircraft
when still a combat pilot, Ben Bennions shot down a
VF110. Watching the battle from the ground was a
thirteen-year-old boy, Bill Maynall. Years later, in 1958,
Ben Bennions and Bill Maynall met and became firm
friends. In that same year Bill Maynall became the
National Air Racing Champion. He had also become a
pilot and developed a passion for flying. This passion he
now shares with Ben Bennions, and they are now often
seen together, as a team, flying an aerobatic Tiger Moth
biplane at air displays.

Taking to the air again means more to Ben Bennions
than just reliving an old life. It is more than nostalgia.
Latterly, he has found peace, tranquillity that has helped
him recover from a breakdown. And initially Ben Bennions needed to regain respect for himself.

In a sense, by getting shot down, Bennions felt that he
had failed. While his injuries were dealt with by Sir
Archibald McIndoe and his team, and his face was
repaired, he needed to find a way to save the other face.
'It's not the exterior face that one's trying to save. It's the
inner feeling of self-sufficiency there. A face-saving
device, if you like. Acceptance of having been shot down
and recovery from having been hurt and having caused so
many other people so much trouble.'

One of Sir Archibald McIndoe's sayings was that the
privilege of dying for one's country was not equal to
the privilege of living for it. As a schoolboy, Bennions

thought that heroes were the men who had died for their country. But McIndoe taught him to think beyond that – even though 'living for one's country' when you're burned and broken was often a harder thing to do.

Ben Bennions, flier extraordinary, has lived for his country.

Jimmy Wright

1 In the beginning: the first photograph of the Club's first committee. From left to right: Tom Gleave, Geoffrey Page, Russell Davies, Peter Weeks, Bill Towers-Perkins, Michael Coote, Sir Archibald McIndoe (p. 14).

2 The surgeon off-duty: Sir Archibald at the piano at an early reunion.

3 Christmas in Ward Three, 1941.

4 The 'Heath Robinson contraption', the saline bath McIndoe introduced to ease the airmen's burns (p. 25).

5 Rehabilitation at Marchwood Park. The Guinea Pig is Australian 'Dusty' Rhodes (p. 33). (Photo: Ian W. Craig)

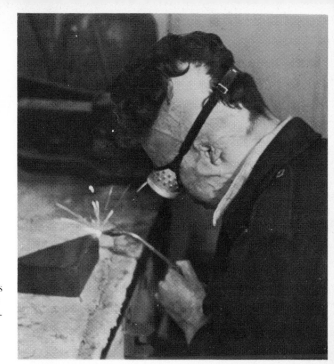

6 Tubby Taylor takes his traditional plunge during the 1978 cocktail party (p. 38). (Photo: Thames Television)

7 Geoffrey Page, fighter pilot (p. 47).

8 Surgeon Guinea Pig Bertram Owen Smith talks during the filming of the Thames Television documentary in 1978 (p. 70). (Photo: Thames Television)

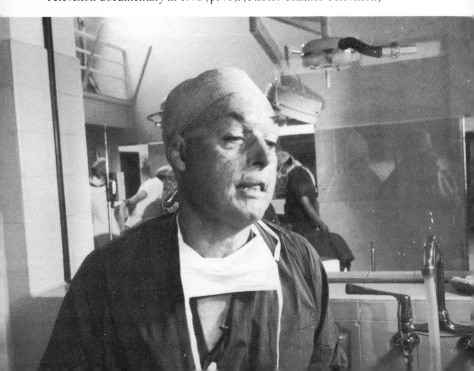

9 'Ben' Bennions at the controls of a Tiger Moth during a Shuttleworth Collection display in 1978 (p. 78). (Photo: Roger Perry, *The Sunday Times*)

10 The Duke of Edinburgh, President of the Guinea Pig Club, talks to Mr and Mrs Jimmy Wright and a patient featured in one of Jimmy Wright's productions, a film about disabled people (p. 86). (Photo: Roger Perry, *The Sunday Times*)

11 Overseas Guinea Pigs Freeman Strickland and Ken Gilkes replace the restaurant sign borrowed during a 1950s' Weekend. On the right is Sir Archibald McIndoe (p. 141). (Photo: Ian W. Craig)

12 Farewell party for two sisters of the Queen Victoria Hospital during the 1970s. From left to right, back row: Tim Walshe, Reg Hyde, Henry Standen, Jack Allaway. Front row: Jackie Hutchinson, Sister Mary Rae, Sister Edna Hitchin, Jimmy Wright, Bill Foxley.

OPPOSITE PAGE
13 Reg Hyde and 'Jock' Tosh at the 1978 reunion (p. 128). (Photo: Thames Television)

14 Ann Shelton sings the songs of the 1940s to the Guinea Pigs of 1978 (p. 129). (Photo: Thames Television)

15 Lady Connie McIndoe at the 1978 Weekend (p. 133). (Photo: Roger Perry, *The Sunday Times*)

16 Chief Guinea Pig Tom Gleave speaks at the 1978 reunion. On his right is guest of honour, Lord Mayor of London Sir Peter Vanneck (p. 132). (Photo: Roger Perry, *The Sunday Times*)

8

Jimmy Wright

They forecast for Jimmy Wright a promising career in the film industry. That was before he joined up. In 1942, he became an aerial photographer and film cameraman in the RAF and, as a result of a plane crash in Italy, the following year he was blinded. Despite this, despite the fact that he was injured to the point of death, he pursued his chosen career and has become a much respected film producer.

In a nutshell, the story of Jimmy Wright is so remarkable it is almost unbelievable. Told at greater length the story is equally remarkable, but less improbable as the character of the man emerges.

The Guinea Pig Club is proud of Jimmy Wright. Talk to any member of the Club about their own and their collective achievements and, before long, you will be asked: 'Have you met Jimmy Wright yet?' One of the unofficial rules of membership of the Club is that you do not boast of your own achievements. It is quite permitted, however, to boast about the achievements of fellow Guinea Pigs.

Wright joined the RAF at the age of nineteen. For the previous two years, he had worked for Technicolor in the camera department. He started work as clapper boy, but with an evident flair for photography and a father who was a respected cameraman, he flourished. Technicolor at the time were making films for the Admiralty and for air gunnery training, but Jimmy's work was not restricted to helping convey wartime facts. One set of photographs in the family album show him working on the set of a period costume film.

If Jimmy Wright had to go to war, he was keen to get into the RAF film unit. He took the photographic course. He started operational flying in Britain, being based in Norfolk, and took part in several operations over the Low Countries. In 1943 he was posted to the Mediterranean area. He went from North Africa to Malta to Sicily and eventually to Italy, as the Allies pushed up through Europe. In his forty-three missions, he remembers a few hair-raising moments; he doesn't disguise the fact that he was 'anxious' when his aircraft was over the target area. As well as taking military pictures, Wright found time to take advantage of being in places he'd never seen before; he produced a fine series of pictures of the volcano, Mount Etna.

His active service as a cameraman ended suddenly. The aircraft, in which he was flying, caught fire on take-off. The fire in the engine was not spotted until the aircraft was airborne. It was too late to stop and there was insufficient height for the crew to bale out. The plane crashed and exploded. Jimmy was amidships and he and another crew member, in the tail of the plane, were the only two survivors. Wright believes he was trapped and eventually dragged out by an American who saved his life. But as he was unconscious, he has no memory of it himself. The registrar at Taranto hospital was so convinced that Jimmy Wright would not survive twenty-four hours that he posted him as dead along with the other members of the crew who had died. His mother received the telegram that her son was dead.

At that time, Jimmy Wright was fighting for his life in an Italian hospital. 'I didn't know where I was. I was drifting, only partly conscious. I was in a totally different world; in fact, I thought I was being tortured in a prisoner-of-war camp.' Because of the pain? 'Yes. And because of the foreign voices, the Italian voices, as the stretcher bearers took me to and from the theatre for treatment. I imagined I'd been captured and they were trying to make me talk. . . . '

His father, by coincidence, was in Italy at the time as a

war correspondent. He heard about the accident and came quickly to the hospital. He asked for the morphine doses to be relaxed so that he could talk to his son and, on the second day after the accident, Jimmy Wright regained consciousness for a brief spell for the first time. For six weeks, he was delirious as he was transferred to two other hospitals, eventually ending at a hospital in a converted school on the Adriatic coast. It was only there that he came into the hands of a medical team who were experienced in dealing with burns. First, his right hand was saved by grafting around the wrist. Then grafts were put on his face and left eye, which was the lesser damaged eye, for uncovered eyes develop corneal ulcers, and the sight goes. At that time, Jimmy Wright had good light perception, but his face was completely bandaged with just a small opening for his mouth, through which his food was pushed. At that stage, Jimmy didn't know how much he could see. It was not until much later that he realised that he could not see at all.

Three months after the crash Jimmy Wright came back to England and to East Grinstead. McIndoe looked at him and gave him his assessment: that he would need four years of extensive plastic surgery to rebuild his face and eyelids. Then, there was a good chance of being able to give him corneal grafts.

The plastic surgery went according to plan. But treating the eyes proved considerably more difficult. Jimmy Wright had been registered as a blind person during the summer of 1944. But he was still sure, in his own mind, that his sight would be restored. At the very least, he believed he would be able to see again with his left eye. He saw many prominent eye surgeons and was given to understand that he had a good chance. The retina, he was told, was working perfectly; it was the cornea which was scarred, letting through no light. Seven attempts were made to give Jimmy Wright a new cornea in the left eye. Each time, there were complications. It was eventually decided to give it a rest, as Wright had already had many dozens of operations. 'I kept a count in the early days. Now, I can only estimate that it must have been between seventy and eighty operations altogether. . . . '

While he waited, Jimmy Wright began to learn the skills to cope with being blind. He was taught braille and now has such an extensive braille filing system in his own office at home, that anyone phoning him would have no idea that he was handicapped. He is able to retrieve names, telephone numbers and addresses in a matter of seconds from the braille cards in boxes in front of him. As Wright began to meet others who had lost their sight, he started to become accustomed to this different way of life.

When each successive eye operation failed, he experienced various emotions. He felt at times that he just wanted to stop the operations, to give up and adapt to a life without sight. But the thought of getting back sight and achieving again a normal working life was seductive even in those moments of despair.

Was he helped by the Ward Three atmosphere? Did he share his experiences with other people? 'Sharing was very largely the driving force. One always met someone who was that much worse off and perhaps in more pain than oneself and this was the reason why everyone just pressed on. You simply couldn't give up . . . . '

Remembering Jimmy Wright in those days of despair and remembering the agonies faced by other Guinea Pigs who had been blinded, Blackie considers that the intensity of realising that you are blind is greater than coming to terms with any other disability.

> If you have a badly burned pair of hands, if you have a badly burned face, and then in the course of your treatment you have to face the fact that you are never going to see again; that moment, I can think of nothing worse . . . .
> In a situation like that there must be a temptation even to end one's life. That thought has certainly

occurred to more than one Guinea Pig, because so
much of what you previously relied on has been
taken from you and through no fault of your own.
But it's at those times when the bond of friendship
and the brotherhood of being with someone upon
whom you can rely, and in an atmosphere which
builds up your faith, is all important. You don't
actually take your life, and thank God, as far as
I know, no Guinea Pig has deliberately taken his
life.

Jimmy Wright had been ambitious. He had had plans to
go and work in an American studio. Now, he was blind.
To work in Hollywood was obviously no longer possible.
Did he feel any bitterness towards the Germans?
Before the war at the age of fourteen he had been on a
cycling holiday to Germany, staying at Youth Hostels. He
met several Germans of his own age and one in particular
became a pen friend. After the war he had a letter from
him. The German friend was in desperate need and was
asking for help, for clothing or food. It was only eighteen
months after the crash. Jimmy Wright says: 'I'm afraid I
didn't reply. I just did not want to have anything to do
with Germans any more. I'm sorry now, because I have
lost complete touch and it would be nice to know how he
and his family are. Whether they survived . . . . '
It would seem impossible for a blinded man to build a
career in the film industry but this is what Jimmy Wright
set out to do. When he finally left hospital in 1951, a
friend who had been with him in the RAF film unit asked
if he would like to join in forming a small film production company. He had been visiting them in between
his operations, although not playing an active part in
film making, and he felt there was a role he might play.
He went to live in Shepperton and started work
at the Shepperton studios. He had to learn a completely
new job. He had known about film making from behind the camera; now, he had to learn production administration. He doubted if he would be able to pull his

weight in the business, but he wanted to try. He needed to try.

He joined the company. To begin with, business was slow. Theirs was a new company and they were struggling to become known. But they made a film for a well-known company and then another. Things began to improve. Commercial television started, and thanks to their experience in producing advertising films for the cinema, they were in a strong position to make television commercials. Much of his work was done on the telephone and until production was under way few clients realised that they were dealing with a blind man.

Then, as now, Jimmy Wright has had to trust his director and cameraman to advise him. His strength has been co-ordination and production administration and, as well as being involved in producing commercials, he has produced documentaries both for business clients and for more general release. He has recently been working on two films on the subject of disablement.

From the moment a film idea is hatched, Wright is the backbone of the production team. He visits the client and discusses the project in detail. He advises on the type of film, the style, the proposed length, the number of locations and, once he has a clear idea what the film is to be like, he calls in a script writer. He next gives the client an idea of the cost of the production, a draft treatment and, if there's agreement, he goes ahead and produces the script.

To assemble the film crew, he relies on past experience. He has worked with a number of technicians on a regular basis, knows the cameramen who are specialists in the various types of film work, and has a wide range of contacts – although he prefers to work with the same, basic nucleus of people. In his braille filing system, he has such details as names of the equipment companies, sound recording companies and recording theatres because when shooting is complete, he must book the recording and dubbing facilities. His secretary keeps the diary and he keeps day-to-day notes on a braille shorthand machine.

His most important and valuable piece of equipment, however, is his own memory.

Jimmy Wright also has a second job, a voluntary one. Early in 1978, he became involved in discussions about producing a local talking newspaper for the blind. He is now chairman of *The Talking News* and arranges the weekly recording sessions. Using a team of thirty or so volunteer readers, and the services of a friend from his RAF film unit days, who is now in charge of the dubbing theatre at Shepperton studios, he produces a cassette of news and feature articles, lasting an hour and a half. The editor of one of the local papers collates the news and, late every Thursday afternoon, just as the local paper goes to press, *The Talking News* team gathers in the recording studios. One side of the cassette is normally devoted to news items and the other side to feature articles, sports news and other items of interest. Sometimes one of the presenters has been out during the week recording a local activity, a local play perhaps. One hundred and thirty cassettes go out each week and machines are supplied to anybody who does not have a recorder of his own. The whole operation is financed by local organisations: Rotary, Round Table, Lions Clubs and so on, and as chairman of *Talking News,* Jimmy Wright has sometimes to go and explain the activities to these organisations – something which, he says, he's slowly getting used to.

It might come as a surprise that a handicapped man, with problems enough in coping with his own job, can find time to devote energies to helping others. But this man is a Guinea Pig, belonging to a Club whose creed is to help one another. Not so surprising, then, that this willingness to see problems and solve them spills over into the outside world.

Guinea Pigs help each other, in most cases simply by keeping in touch with each other. There are, of course, funds available for Guinea Pigs in special need – and Tom Gleave, Blackie, Bernard Arch and Russell Davies are there if needed. But to Jimmy Wright the value of being

a Guinea Pig is being able to meet other Guinea Pigs.
And the most important event of the year is of course
the Lost Weekend at East Grinstead. It is a time for
caring and sharing and for replenishing self-confidence.
'Archie McIndoe instilled that confidence in us. He used
to say nothing was impossible – it simply takes a little bit
longer.'

9

Sam Gallop

To talk to Sam Gallop for any length of time is to begin to understand what it's like to be disabled. Not that Sam is obviously disabled at all. Unlike most Guinea Pigs, his face seems unmarked. Only later do you discover that it was crushed and totally rebuilt. Certainly he walks a little stiffly. Only if you ask will he tell you that he has artificial legs.

Sam Gallop, RAF pilot, university graduate, sharp of mind and feature, has devoted much of his energy in the last thirty years to convincing the rest of the world that they should not forget the needs of the disabled.

However magnificent the building, if the door's too narrow to take a wheelchair, a certain small percentage of people won't ever be able to get into it. Which is unfair.

However wonderful the view, if there's no lift big enough to accommodate the disabled, this same small percentage won't be able to scale the mountain to share the experience. Which is also unfair.

And it needs only a little thinking time, at the planning stage, to remedy the situation and prevent the disabled feeling like second-class citizens. After all, nobody *asks* to be disabled.

For instance, I was coming into land in bad weather and another aircraft flew up my backside, it was nobody's fault.

Thus Gallop describes the moment on Easter Sunday,

Sam Gallop

1943, when, quite involuntarily, he became a member of the Guinea Pig Club. Following the impact, he came down from a thousand feet in a controlled dive, his aircraft hit the ground and blew up. His life was saved by an Air Force Corporal and a jeep-load of Americans who, despite the flames, managed to drag him to safety. When an Air Force doctor arrived, Sam Gallop was lying outside the aircraft, with his eyes wide open but unconscious. He had minor brain damage, broken upper and lower jaws, he had knocked out his teeth, injured his left arm, lost a finger on his left hand, had various burns all over his body and his shoes were burned away. His legs were broken 'in all directions' and as a result both lower legs needed to be amputated. He had also injured his back.

The next eighteen months Sam Gallop remembers as a succession of trips to the operating table. They seemed never ending. Regaining consciousness seven days after the accident, he remembers being totally confident in everything that was being done for him. The most important task was to get his legs fit enough to take artificial limbs. He hated the wheelchair. He became very frustrated at not being able to walk. He cared less about his face, though he knew it needed considerable recon-struction. He also remembers the moment when it would have been easier to die than to fight on. It happened in the middle of the night. He was lying in bed and looking out of the window at the stars.

> I had a curious feeling that it was not as noisy in the corridor outside as it had been; I felt I could have wafted gently away. It was a curious feeling of being outside myself, looking down at myself and feeling that if it weren't for the people walking up and down outside in the corridor, keeping the world turning over, I could easily have made my excuses and left.

Sam Gallop had seventeen operations altogether. As the weeks became months, so Sam Gallop's eagerness for the challenge grew. He won a university place. He joined the

Central Electricity Generating Board. He learned about being disabled. And he points to pitfalls that have been avoided.

First, he believes the Guinea Pigs could have been throttled by too much sympathy. For sympathy can be a dangerous thing.

> When you're in a hospital bed, a warm tender feeling coming to you from the girl who is nursing you, and from the doctor, is essential to recovery. If you are feeling ghastly and you are given the right treatment, by being shaved and sat up in bed, you can look around and take a fresh view of life. After that, however, sympathy has got to be rather subtle.
>
> It is very difficult for those responsible for rehabilitation to stand back from the people they are trying to help, and hold back their own feelings of sympathy and concern. They mustn't wallow in sympathy. They should decide matters almost dispassionately if that's possible. I am afraid that a lot of the energy that goes into caring would be far better converted into the energy of effective action. People care but they don't see. They don't see the real need and I think it is the patient, more than anyone else, who has to help them to see.

Excessive concern, Sam Gallop believes, could destroy a Guinea Pig's self-confidence. He would become dependent, whereas the aim should be to make him independent. The secret of the Guinea Pig Club, more than anything else, has been that by their irreverent attitude towards each other's disabilities, they have helped each other. From the outside, the attitude seems almost cruel. From the inside, it was necessary.

> If somebody moaned, 'Oh my God, I'm in pain this morning,' the automatic reaction would be, 'Oh Jesus, you'll have me in tears on the carpet in a minute.' It wasn't as callous as it sounds, but it was

the right reaction in that place, at that time. It would be a little tricky if someone tried this from outside the Club. You might get thrown out on your ear . . . .

There is a real sense in which you have to be disabled to understand what being disabled is about.

Being disabled means that life, inevitably, is riddled with frustrations. Many of them are unnecessary in a world that still to a large degree ignores the needs of the handicapped. For example, steps are still put into buildings quite unnecessarily – and it still happens that a building, designed with disabled people in mind, welcomes its first wheelchair tenant only to have her blocked by a step on the way to the main entrance.

> There was the classic case of the lady in the wheelchair who went to a hotel which was very proud of its suite containing a full wheelchair toilet and bathroom facility. Unfortunately, she had to send for a carpenter to take the door off the bathroom because somebody had forgotten that the bathroom door took an inch off the access so that the wheelchair couldn't quite get through.
>
> I think it would be good for most professional people, as part of their training, to experience a week – and I do mean a week; a solid seven days and nights in their bedroom as well – in a wheelchair, imagining that they had lost the use of their legs. I think we would see tremendous improvements.

Putting his thoughts into practice, Sam Gallop has been vetting the City of London's facilities for the disabled.

Gallop remembers with pleasure the attitude of the authorities during his three years at Oxford. Though the college may not have been designed for the disabled, the college staff exhibited a refreshing willingness to adapt. They did not discuss his disability. They did not discuss how he was going to get into the college. They left it entirely to him to work out how he got in and out of the buildings, assuming that he would use his intelligence and come and talk to them if change was necessary. Fortunately, he could drive his car virtually to the front door of the college. He had to go back to hospital regularly for check ups, both on himself and on his artificial legs, and the Dons were very understanding. He would just stick his head round the door and say, 'I'm terribly sorry my strap has broken', or, 'I've got a scar, I must pop up to town for half a day', and they would say, 'By all means, go.' He recognised that this was special treatment. Undergraduates were supposed to stay in Oxford and not go to London. But then, just sometimes, rules are there to be broken. . . .

By a coincidence, when Sam Gallop applied for a post in the Electricity Supply industry, he found himself being interviewed by another limbless person. Instead of discussing the job, they talked of the difficulties of driving a car without hand controls. And, at the end of it all, Gallop was told he had the job. 'Perhaps the other people on the board were fascinated by the conversation . . . . '

Yet from government statistics, it can be seen that employers of disabled people are in the minority. Sam Gallop claims not even the Department of Employment itself is employing its full quota of disabled people. 'Perhaps the problem is that there's an inadequate supply of trained disabled people, meaning that firms cannot meet their quota anyway. But, if that's the case, why isn't more being done about increasing training schemes?'

Sam Gallop takes a complex view of the Guinea Pig Club today. At the least, it means a once-a-year return to East Grinstead.

The minute I cross the 'customs barrier' into East Grinstead, I feel the batteries starting to recharge. It is a happy weekend. It is almost like taking off in an aircraft; I get an emotional surge.

There's nostalgia in the conversations, but it is *not* a nostalgic Club. It's a Club which looks forward. There are problems to be discussed and problems

shared. And people don't perhaps reveal to themselves that they have problems until they get back
into that atmosphere.

One doesn't often like to admit to oneself that one
has certain disabilities until one gets back into that
shared atmosphere. One finds oneself talking in a
more open way and thinking more about what one is
doing with one's life. And what one's aims are, in a
realistic way.

Realism involves recognising when one is battering one's
head against a brick wall, trying for the impossible. A man
with no feet or damaged hands can be trying very hard in
life but there is a point at which perhaps a friend can say
to him, 'Look, you are trying too hard in this area. But try
somewhere else, because you are not going to win this
one.'

It is part of the philosophy of the Club that all Guinea
Pigs should attempt anything if they want to. It is part of
the experience gained by all Guinea Pigs that, as hard as
they try, they may not necessarily succeed. Excellence,
says Gallop, is sometimes unattainable. You may be
disabled, and learn to play golf, but you're never going to
become a scratch golfer. The quicker you recognise that,
the less anguish for everyone.

Sam Gallop, a man with no legs, has just learnt to ride a
horse, but he has no plans to follow Harvey Smith over
the show jumping courses of the world. He recognises his
limitations.

What enabled Sam Gallop to come to terms with his
disabilities?

First the professional help and support of Sir Archibald
McIndoe and the staff at East Grinstead; secondly the
example of other Guinea Pigs. Underlying all this,
however, was the fact that he, along with the other Guinea
Pigs, was made to believe that they were important
people, that they mattered. This was not conveyed to them
directly, it just came out as a general atmosphere, the
general determination to reach higher medical standards.

The Guinea Pigs still feel that they are special. 'Not in a vain way,' Sam Gallop explains.

> They feel that they were given the best treatment in the world, that they had a unique experience and that they have 'enjoyed' that experience. They probably believe too that everybody else in the same boat ought to be made to feel special. Unfortunately, I think this is not the case. We in the Guinea Pig Club were, and are very lucky.

Some Guinea Pigs, however, never turn up at a weekend. Why does Sam Gallop think this is?

> This could be because they are so disabled medically, and I do know of certain cases where they physically cannot get back. But some Guinea Pigs simply don't like 'clubs', the club atmosphere. Then again perhaps total success is if Pigs consider the Club a helpful experience – but you do not go back. You just go forward and you have happy memories of the Guinea Pig Club, but you do not need to go back.

Some Guinea Pigs do not come back because in the intervening year they have died. Sam Gallop feels a sadness not about death but for the man that he hasn't seen for a year who, because of the accumulation of wounds and because of having fought such a very hard physical battle, has suddenly suffered a severe physical decline, because the war time experience is catching up. He does not regard death as a sad experience unless it is painful. To a man who is used to death it is part of the daily round. The sadness is in seeing the war catch up with people who fought very hard over a number of years to conquer their disabilities. It can happen quite suddenly, quite dramatically. People somehow run out of physical steam, says Gallop. 'The war's been over a long time, but the price is still being paid.'

10

Alan Morgan

The most famous hands in Canada, in medical circles at
least, are to be found making precision industrial tools at a
factory near Manchester in England. They belong to Alan
Morgan and derive their transatlantic fame from the work
of the Canadian surgeon Ross Tilley. He was the member
of McIndoe's team who fathomed how to give Alan
Morgan's hands grip and control when it was decided that
his black, frost-bitten, fingers were beyond repair. He was
so proud of his achievement that photographs of Alan's
hands have held pride of place among his lecture slides.

You can see what Tilley did to him the moment Alan
greets you, gripping your hand firmly with his two
re-formed hands. With enough thumb saved to provide
leverage, Morgan's hands have been split between the
bones so that the bones of the hands become fingers. It is
as if the webbing of a duck's foot has been split to free a
set of claws. Alan is unusual as a Guinea Pig in that he
was not burned but frost bitten, not 'fried' – to use the
club's terminology – but 'frozen'.

He was called up at Christmas 1942. Previously he had
been turned down by the Navy, because he'd been in a
reserved occupation. He had trained as an engineer and
was at various times making fixtures for Lancaster bombers and components for Spitfires. He worked well and
hard, there being no shortage of work in wartime.

Soon the need was as much for aircrew as aeroplanes.
Before long, he was flying as flight engineer. He flew on
twelve successful missions. The thirteenth coincided with
his twenty-first birthday. His fiancée Ella, now his wife,

Alan Morgan

will never forget the day: 'He was due his first official
leave for seven months. We prepared everything for a
party. He never turned up. We knew something was
wrong. A telegram went to his parents saying he'd been
injured. But they didn't give any details.'

Over Stuttgart Alan's plane, carrying a full bomb load,
was attacked. The main door was blown open. The
wireless operator went to close it but blacked out.

I remember getting hold of an emergency oxygen
bottle. I went right down to the rear door, found this
body and dragged him back to his position and
plugged him in to his oxygen supply. It was pitch
black.

I then went to close the door. As I was trying to
close it, I blacked out myself. Thank God the skipper
realised what had happened. To give me more
oxygen he had to dive immediately from 20,000 feet
to 8,000 feet. And this was over Stuttgart, remember.
There was a helluva lot of flak [anti-aircraft fire] so it
must have been bad. I remember recovering, but I
was in a dazed state. My hands had been touching
the air frame and I suppose they got really, truly
frost-bitten. It was very, very cold at that height and
I could have been like that, without gloves on for five
minutes perhaps.

He did not realise he had been seriously frost-bitten until
the Lancaster limped back and landed in Britain. He
remembers fumbling with his torch, and seeing the skin
peeling off a hand as the torch rolled away. Alan Morgan
went first to the civilian hospital in Colchester. His fingers
ballooned up. He couldn't bend them. His hands were
dressed in warm saline gloves, unhappily the wrong
treatment. When he was visited by McIndoe and whisked
to East Grinstead, the surgeon immediately put his frozen
hands into ice buckets to thaw out slowly over a period of
ten days. It was too late and the treatment didn't work.

Blackie remembers Alan's fingers as being 'like little

black charcoal biscuits.' He remembers Alan himself, the quiet northern lad as being very nervous, 'not quite knowing what was happening to him. After the operation he needed a lot of support. He didn't believe that people without fingers could do a job. Not only did he finally accept his injury, he became determined to use his hands and live by them.'

Alan's spur in life as he waited for his new hands to heal and harden was to return to the air. It meant promotion as well as proving to himself that he could return to normal life. McIndoe took his ambition seriously, as he did all Guinea Pig ambitions, however outlandish. He sent him to a special medical board who in turn sent him on a navigation course. His months of patient exercise with his hands, learning how to grip and write again, had paid off.

As Morgan took to the air again, it was a major victory, both for him and for East Grinstead. For when he was most desperately ill, most frightened, he was given only a fifty-fifty chance of survival, such was the shock of frost-bite and the weakening effect of the pneumonia which followed.

In his time at East Grinstead, almost a year in all, Alan made many friends. Each year, he arrives in his caravan for the Lost Weekend and parks it in the grounds of Gotwick Manor a little way out of the town, the home of one of his friends and a long-time friend of the club and hospital, Elaine Blond. She is also one of the club's leading benefactors.

After the war, the comforts of East Grinstead and the privileges which go with being a Guinea Pig, Alan returned home to the realities of the industrial north west. He was newly married with new responsibilities.

He and Ella took on a small grocery-cum-confectionery business. The business prospered. Alan's uncle was a cooked meats manufacturer and the Guinea Pig Club helped pull a few strings with the leading tobacco and sweet firms. On good days, there would be queues twenty yards long outside the little main road store.

When the family arrived, Kenneth first and four years
later Peter, the shop proved too much of a burden and
Alan was thrown back on earning all the family income
with his hands; jig boring at the firm where he had
trained – meticulously accurate machine drilling for which
he had a flair. 'At the beginning it was a struggle, but
within six months I was back in the routine.' His biggest
problem, until his hands had toughened sufficiently, was
handling cold materials. 'It was uncomfortable but I never
gave up.'

But why did Alan, like so many other Guinea Pigs
choose the hardest career open to a man without fingers?
Wasn't he ever tempted to go for the soft option?

> It might be a wrong thing to do, but I find I'm always
> out to prove that I can do better than the next man,
> better than somebody with fingers. If there's two
> people on a job, and they're both doing the same
> thing, I always tend to want to do my job quicker and
> better than the other lad, if only to satisfy myself.

That is the challenge of the Guinea Pigs; their philosophy,
but also their weakness. Meeting challenge day in, day out
can produce strain, or at least the inability to cope with
additional strain when it comes along, which is precisely
what happened to Alan Morgan.

He could meet the challenge of work but in 1960 he had
to cope with the pressures of redundancy. Alan and five
hundred workmates became the unlucky pawns in the
game of industrial take-over.

At the start, he thought it would be easy to get a new
job. He was an above-average skilled craftsman, 'but
trying to convince a new boss of that when you're sitting
opposite him at an interview with two deformed hands in
your lap, is another matter.' Employers were not eager to
risk taking on a disabled man when there was no shortage
of fully fit men on the unemployment register.

I went for one job at a bottling firm. They wanted a

toolroom inspector. Now, I could do that job perfectly well, but the personnel manager was more concerned with asking how I would manage a micro-
meter. And then he said the work might be too heavy
for me. He'd put problems in the way.

Then after the interview there was the waiting. I
either got no reply or a letter saying the vacancy had
gone to someone else. I was getting more and more
frustrated.

Ella takes up the story:

They just didn't seem to accept that Alan could do
the job and had been jig boring for seventeen years.

As time went on and there was no new work in
sight, Alan became quiet. He got very depressed.
People it seemed hadn't the confidence in him and
he lost confidence in himself.

I didn't realise how bad things were. I didn't
realise he was not sleeping at nights. When he got a
new job, in the end, he had worked himself up to
such a state that he couldn't manage it. He believed
what the others believed – that he couldn't do it. He
worked ten days but then he was ill.

They were dark days for the normally chirpy Alan. 'It
brought my disability to the front. It made me think that I
was disabled, and really I wasn't.' The illness took a form
which those who have had breakdowns will recognise only
too well. 'I didn't want to go out. Ella had to force me to
go out, even shopping. I was not interested in life. I
wouldn't mix with people.'

Ella had to take command, run the house and slowly, so
slowly, ease and cajole Alan back to his former self. 'Alan
wouldn't take any decisions. He didn't want to know. He
wouldn't go anywhere. I was working part-time and
whenever I came home, and had to go shopping I would
make him come, too.'

Time and love are greater healers. In time Alan was

back at work, but he hadn't learned the lessons of his experience. 'Unfortunately', says Ella, 'he has one failing. He's a perfectionist. If he hadn't been like that he would have coped with the danger of breakdown better.' And perhaps he wouldn't have had his second breakdown.

In a sense, it was my fault again. A friend of mine offered me a good position – a manager's job. I was in charge of twenty-four women on moulding tools. Trying to keep the peace and run the department worried me; I wasn't doing enough. I was responsible, too, for making the tools the women were using. After five weeks the symptoms came back; the sleepless nights. Ella knew I was heading for a breakdown, so I packed up the job. I must have been nine months like that, until I was fully fit again.

By the second time round as an unemployed person Alan had learned from bitter experience. He went for one job as a toolmaker and kept his hands in his pockets for the interview. He got the job.

It was a funny thing but three weeks later, after I'd started the job, the owner of the firm who had given me the job saw me. He said, 'Morgan, you never told me you'd lost your fingers.' I said that I didn't think it was important enough to tell him. But I asked was he satisfied with my work. If he wasn't he could sack me in a month. He must have been satisfied. I stayed there eleven years.

But Alan's one failing, his Guinea Pig-headed determination, is also his strength. If he had not had the determination instilled into him in Ward Three would he have been able to work at all? Perhaps he would have been fit for little more than easy work in a sheltered workshop, rather than being able to take his place with pride in a northern engineering works.

It is Morgan's assertion that there is nothing at work

that he cannot do. No one makes any special allowances for him, except perhaps that Alan is given the jobs which require the greatest skill and care. 'We do jigs and fixtures for all the big companies – Rolls Royce, the RB 211 jigs and fixtures. We make inspection fixtures, turning fixtures, milling fixtures, work for the motor trade, the Ford Motor Company.'

He is proud of his work and its reputation. In his work area at the factory everything is neat and tidy. He has developed a few hand tools of his own to help him with his work. He has also learned that added responsibility and worry over-tax his reserves of determination; living off his hard-won skill is what he excels at.

It would be wrong to leave an impression that Alan Morgan merely lives for his work. He and Ella run a local amateur football team, Woodley Athletic. He's shown his usual adaptability when playing sport. Football was no problem – but cricket was a different matter. In true Guinea Pig spirit, Alan thought about the problem and found a solution. 'I used to have a big, thick band of elastic, tied round my wrist. I twisted it then tied it round the bat.' If everything worked well, Alan could hit fours and sixes. If anything went wrong he'd hit the bowler, with a flying bat.

One final, vital observation: to know the Morgans is to realise that theirs is a good marriage, interests shared, troubles shared. 'I couldn't have done it without my wife' is a phrase of Alan's which occurs often and is sincerely meant. And all the most fortunate Guinea Pigs will echo the sentiment.

11

Bill Warman

Nothing keeps Bill Warman away from the Lost Weekend. He's a gregarious man with a mischievous sense of
humour and a great liking for parties. The weekend is the
climax of the year for him. He has missed only one since
the war. He ticks off the days on the calendar as the
weekend approaches. He lives and savours every one of
the weekend's activities to the full and returns home each
year, feeling a little flat that it's all over, for another twelve
months. However, there's always next year to look forward to . . . .

'Home' is a neat house in a pleasant, unpretentious side
road in Finchley, north London. Outside his home is
parked a spotless saloon car, Bill Warman's great pride.
He works part-time as a carhire driver to supplement his
disablement pension. One Saturday he might be at a
wedding, driving bride and groom from the church, the
next week driving a customer to the airport.

Bill Warman became a member of the Guinea Pig Club
as the result of something as simple as a faulty tyre on the
Stirling in which he was flying as flight engineer. When
the aircraft hit the ground it burst into flames. Bill
Warman remembers the sound of ammunition exploding
and the long wait for help.

The next three or four weeks of his life are just a hazy
memory. He had an emergency operation to give him new
eyelids to prevent the eyes becoming ulcerated. He
remembers the long, painful treatment of his other burns.
His mind had a strange mixture of impressions, questions
to mull over. When the aircraft crashed, it broke up. Bill

Bill Warman

Warman survived while the man sitting next to him was killed outright. Why had fate spared Bill Warman? During the ride in the ambulance, Warman asked the driver if his face was burnt. 'It's not touched, mate, there's not a mark on it,' came the reply. This automatic reply was meant to bring comfort. . . .

He knew he was badly burned, but the full force of the remark hit him strongly only when, one day in the ward, he chanced to see his reflection in the side of a gleaming sterilising urn. It would be an understatement to say it came as a shock, but Bill Warman adds quickly, 'In theory you're living in your own little world where all you're concerned about is Number One. But then you look around at the other chaps and realise just how lucky you are.' Again the litany: there's always someone worse off than you are. . . .

In due course, McIndoe brought Warrant Officer Warman to East Grinstead. There was a lot of work to be done to his face and hands, as the scars today attest. He spent six months in Ward Three before being transferred to the Canadian Wing.

The hospital was quite classless, he recalls. 'Pain is a great leveller. But amazingly enough, the experience was a lot of fun and I wouldn't have missed it for the world.'

In Bill Warman's day the close bond between East Grinstead and the Guinea Pigs' hospital was well formed. McIndoe and the pioneer Pigs had done the ground work. Away from the town, Bill Warman often found a different attitude.

In Eastbourne one afternoon we were just going into a cafe for a cup of tea when a dear old lady stopped us, looked at our plasters and bandages and asked, 'Has there been an explosion?' You're pretty sensitive about things at that time and it's hard to explain – or even to want to bother to explain . . . .

And, once, on the train from London I was asleep and a lady woke me up to ask what had happened to my ear. I said that I promised my wife that I would

do anything for her and she called my bluff and said,
'Well, cut your right ear off', which I did.

The reaction of the lady is not recorded, but Bill swears
the story is true.

In all, Bill Warman has had around thirty operations.
As well as the plastic surgery he has been in and out of
other hospitals for treatment. He developed various inter-
nal problems as a result of the crash, having swallowed
some fuel. Bill Warman's life subsequently has been
dogged by ill-health. Yet whatever the medical obstacles,
the McIndoe declaration holds firm. Every Guinea Pig
should become a full and useful member of society. It's
just that, in some cases it seems harder than others.

Bill Warman admits things have not always gone
smoothly. He and the Club have shared an uphill struggle.

I had a probationary spell with Marks and Spencer.
But I found the retail world wasn't for me. In any
case, it was no escape from uniforms!

I had visions of starting a car hire business and
probably, one day having a fleet of motor cars. But,
somehow, it hasn't worked out that way. Unfortunately, I had a lot of bad health which retarded my
ambition.

I built up a reputation in a small way. I built it up
through punctuality and service. But when I had
these fairly long periods of illness, things began to
slide. I used to delegate my work to other people,
who perhaps didn't have the same personal interest
that I had. Obviously something must go, something
must suffer.

He doesn't enjoy driving so much today.

The car hire business is entirely different. I used to
drive granny, mother and grandchildren and they
would confide in me. Tell me things they wouldn't
tell their best friend. I had a great interest in the job.

Today, with the mini-cabs and so on, the emphasis is
a lot less on the sort of service I was offering.

The business never made huge profits. Many years, it lost
money. The costs – tax, insurance and maintenance – were
high. There was never any money left to finance expan-
sion. Often, a replacement car was beyond Bill Warman's
reach when his vehicle reached the end of its useful life.

Warman admits he's a worrier. The worry did not
improve his health. He also worried about the quality of
his service. Like so many other Guinea Pigs, he wanted to
prove he was as good as the next man. His work is limited
now, as there is a ceiling on his earnings because he
receives a disablement pension on which to live.

How has the accident affected his ability to achieve? Bill
Warman feels he should have done better in life:

When I was young I did feel bitter. Perhaps more
angry with myself, than bitter. I'm that much older
now, and I accept it. But I wish I'd never gone into
the car hire business. As the years have gone by, I've
come to the realisation that I shan't get very far now,
not a man of my age.

I haven't exactly made a mark in the world, have
I?

I now live from day to day and accept the fact that
I am what I am, and that's all.

I would have attempted to have sought other
employment some time ago, a good many years ago,
but I have not been well. And, to be frank, I don't
think I would be a good risk to employ.

I have never, I repeat never, played on my injuries.
I found no reason to. I've had help from people. The
Guinea Pig Club and the RAF Benevolent Fund
who have been very very good.

And when I've needed the Guinea Pig Club,
they've always been there. A major repair on my car,
perhaps which I couldn't pay, and the Club and the
Fund would pay the bill. Or when my car insurance

became due, which is fairly high, they would help me
in that way. I can pick up the telephone any time I
want to get advice or help from any of our committee
members.

A phone call to Bernard Arch, or to Blackie, in his
London office at Sotheby's or in his home on the outskirts
of Barnstaple in north Devon: supporting Guinea Pigs
financially has been part of the Club's brief from the
beginning. Blackie says:

> We started out by supporting Guinea Pigs anony-
> mously; by supporting the firms that employed them
> because they were not able to earn a full salary. But
> we didn't want them to be given charity. Or to be
> seen to be given charity. They earned a full wage
> and, gradually, we reduced our input. We have
> considerable help from the RAF Benevolent Fund,
> who have always accepted the principle that all
> should be helped according to their need.

Blackie sees Bill Warman as an individualist.

> Well liked by all his colleagues but we couldn't think
> how to resettle him. He didn't want to, he couldn't
> have been seen working in a factory. Not only is he
> badly burned but he swallowed a lot of petrol – he's
> hardly any guts at all – and finally we decided that
> what he needed to do was to be a car hire driver. We
> bought him a car and then we renewed his car, and
> we're constantly supporting and helping him when
> he comes to the end of his tether in any way. And
> this applies to a whole lot of other Guinea Pigs.

To Bill Warman, the Club is 'the be all and end all of
everything'. Around the walls in his home are souvenirs
and mementos. He has even kept the grisly medical
photographs of his skin grafts, mounted on a piece of now

fading card. Many of his friends are Guinea Pigs. Bernard Arch lives nearby and so does Guinea Pig Vic Hobbs, who was so determined to use his hands after his injuries and return to his job in the electricity industry that he spent hour after hour making intricate models.

Comradeship is a key element in the Club. 'A fellow Pig will understand you just a little more than somebody else will, and you'll understand him. You'll listen to him, he'll listen to you. Perhaps I will learn something from him.'

What has Bill Warman learned from being a Guinea Pig apart from recognising pain with all its pitfalls and what it feels like to have the ambitions of youth thwarted? He says tolerance, understanding, the acceptance of disability and humour. For humour is what Bill Warman gives back to the Club. He can't boast he has been a great success in the material sense. He hasn't been a top executive, he hasn't become a plastic surgeon or a film producer, but he has retained his Londoner's wit. Bill Warman finds the wisecrack which turns Guinea Pig gatherings into parties. The Club would be poorer without him.

Reg Hyde

12

Reg Hyde

Crawley New Town is a maze of neat roads. Follow them
through to the little village of Ifield which merges with the
new estates on the western side. On a sharp bend in the
road there is the old church of St Margaret's. Here, one
windy March afternoon in 1979, there was one of the
biggest gatherings of Guinea Pigs ever outside a Lost
Weekend. They had come to pay tribute to one of their
number, Guinea Pig Reg Hyde.

The Church was packed, not just with Guinea Pigs. Reg
Hyde was a highly respected member of the community.
In life he was the man responsible for planning, building
and maintaining many of the roads along which his
friends and colleagues had driven to reach the church.
Until three years before, Reg Hyde had been executive
engineer at Crawley, a position he reached with character-
istic Guinea Pig determination after suffering appalling
burns and undergoing one of the longest programmes of
medical treatment of any Club member.

At the height of his career, Reg Hyde was a man with
an exceptional memory. He would retain details in his
mind which most other people would need to search for in
their filing systems. His interest in planning was avid. He
went to America, where he studied bridges, roads and
out-of-town developments, constantly searching for ideas
to bring back to Crawley. The town is a monument to Reg
Hyde's diligence and inspiration.

Then, three years ago, his life began to change. His wife
Jean began to notice that he was not taking the interest he
used to, in his job and surroundings. 'At home, normally,

he would sit and have masses of books around him, asking questions and solving problems. Then gradually, he began to deteriorate, to forget things, to have difficulty in expressing himself. . . . '

In his final months, Reg Hyde had reached the point where walking, speaking and eating were difficult. He retired prematurely. He did little more than sit all day watching television and could be left for no more than an hour or two at a time. In 1978 he missed the Guinea Pig Reunion Dinner and Annual General Meeting; he was able to come only for a short while to the cocktail party on Sunday. The Guinea Pigs were delighted to see him, but their delight was mingled with sadness and worry, for the Reg Hyde who sat in the hospital grounds, at the cocktail party, listening to his friends but saying little, was not the sharp-witted man of old . . . .

Reg became a Guinea Pig while training others to fly Wellington bombers. At the end of the trip, just before landing, the port engine stopped. Automatically Reg took up the crash-landing position. The aircraft was over the runway and Reg Hyde expected a bumpy landing and no more. However, there was another aircraft on the runway and there was no way in which the pilot could increase power and make a second attempt at landing. They avoided the other aircraft but crash landed. Ironically, Reg would have been on the other aircraft had he not changed seats that night with the other navigator.

The Wellington hit two trees and Reg Hyde, wearing neither his gloves nor helmet, found himself in the middle of a blazing aircraft. The astrodome was jammed. With superhuman strength, which Hyde has never understood, he forced himself free. Blinded by the fire, he jumped on to one of the torn off wings, and found himself up to his knees in flames. He knew he had to get away before the plane exploded. He climbed clear of the wing, pushed his way through a barbed wire fence and fell into a ditch.

He spent month after long month in hospital. At first he could hardly open his mouth and had to be fed through a tube. It was not until he was transferred to East Grinstead that his mouth was sufficiently restored for him to be able to eat.

In all, Reg Hyde had about eighty operations. Many of them were unsuccessful as the grafts did not take. The study of tissue-matching was still in its infancy, and Reg Hyde was in a serious condition. From the operations Hyde underwent and which failed, knowledge was built up. This was the start of East Grinstead becoming one of the world's most advanced tissue-matching centres. At the time the long-term effects of anaesthesia were unknown. Even today there is little way of being able to quantify the cumulative effect of anaesthesia. John Hunter and Russell Davies knew that with every new operation Guinea Pigs like Reg Hyde were entering uncharted territory.

The Guinea Pigs were entering the unknown in another sense. They were given a new confidence and determination to enable them to go out into society. They used the Ward Three 'overdrive' to win their place in society. But how long was the overdrive designed to last? How long can a Guinea Pig keep up the momentum? What happens if the momentum fails?

Reg's widow, Jean, as a nurse, appreciates the argument that eighty operations and eighty anaesthetics can possibly have had a delayed effect. She also accepts as probable that the years of striving by an injured man to regain his place in society can take their toll in the end. But just how hard it was for her husband to regain and keep his place in society is something Jean Hyde admits she does not know. He never complained. He worked long hours to gain his qualifications, being allowed only one concession by the examining board, a little extra time to get his answers on to paper because of the difficulty he experienced in writing.

To return to happier days: Jean and Reg Hyde met at East Grinstead. Jean Fuggle was staff nurse in the recovery ward. After every operation the Guinea Pigs spent a night in the recovery ward under observation, and Reg Hyde was there after one of his many. Jean had been in London for the day and had just gone on duty. She

was amazed when the second patient she went to, not a
man she knew, said 'Hello, Jean'.

> I said, 'How did you know my name?' and he said,
> 'Well, I'll tell you. The Marchioness of Carisbrooke
> (who'd nursed me in the Canadian wing) said you
> should look out for Jean.' From there on he started
> talking.
>   He'd had a graft, a facial graft, a routine one. The
> next day he came back to recovery and we started
> going out together and that's how it all started.

About a year later they married. Their marriage Jean
describes as having been normal, happy with the usual
ups and down. They had three children. While his injuries
did not hinder him in his work until the final years, there
were some practical things around the house which called
for compromise. He used to have to call Jean to help him
if a screw needed to be put in. 'We battled on, and I
became quite a handy-woman.' There were extra pressures on Jean inevitably. 'It was no good me going in
complaining of a headache, feeling awful or anything like
that, because I've found one was expected to accept that
sort of thing.'

In the last months the pressures on Jean grew steadily.
She had a full-time job as a nurse at Gatwick Airport and
despite friends and relations helping with Reg, she often
found she returned from a night shift to face a day with
only a few snatches of sleep, looking after Reg, before
returning to the airport to work. Exhaustion followed her
like a shadow.

She has had to make a tremendous readjustment in the
last three years. Shortly before Reg's death, she said,
'After you've had somebody very agile, mentally, it's very
difficult to accept them as they are now.' In his final
weeks, Reg lost his speech as well. He died peacefully at
the beginning of March.

What does she feel about the price she and Reg have
had to pay? It is not something she has ever talked about.

She considers they have been lucky. Reg might have been killed and they might have missed their thirty years together. And she sees it as an advantage that Reg was a member of the Guinea Pig Club. If he had been injured in another way or been in the Army or Navy he would have had none of the advantages of membership. The Club helped with the education of their children and was always poised, ready to help, should the need arise.

Yet, at the end, every day was a struggle. Even if Reg was in hospital for a spell, Jean had little time for rest. She was on the move travelling from Ifield to London to visit him. It took Jean many hours of soul searching before deciding to talk openly about the Reg's decline. His story was one of struggle and achievement with a dash of romance thrown in. Why spoil it by telling the world about the last three years?

It was when watching the television programme *Holocaust* that she decided it would be wrong to hide anything. Not every Guinea Pig story could have a happy ending. They are all fighting every day to preserve their self respect and to overcome their handicaps. They are still fighting the war – not against the Germans but against the difficulties of everyday life.

Watching *Holocaust,* a programme about Hitler's treatment of the Jews, Jean says she realised that the new generation should not be allowed to forget the horrors which she and her generation had experienced in order to achieve victory. And who will argue with Jean Hyde when she says: 'It is essential that the world should know such things happened, and what Reg and his comrades did for their country. The price they have paid should not be forgotten.'

Noel Newman

13

Noel Newman

Noel Newman was one of the very last to join the exclusive Guinea Pig Club. He was 'fried' in North Africa in 1945 on his way to Naples to become senior medical officer at the airport.

He is an unusual Guinea Pig. He was not aircrew, but an RAF doctor. He was ten years older than most of the other Pigs he found on arrival at East Grinstead and was 'very bucked to be asked to join the club'.

He had joined up in 1942, having previously been a junior surgical registrar at St Batholemew's Hospital, at Rochester in Kent. As with all junior doctors, he found himself 'working the clock through', but when he did find time to reflect on his future plans he had no doubt that he wanted to be a surgeon. It came therefore as a great blow to learn after his crash that his most crucial injuries were to his hands. His legs were also broken and his body burned and he had head injuries, but it was his hands which caused him the most distress.

To begin with McIndoe exuded optimism. 'We'll have you right in a few weeks,' he told 'Doc' Newman. But strangely it did not matter that this optimism proved worthless. Noel Newman took three and a half years to recover, but 'even as the treatment went on and on, somehow I never lost faith'. Looking back on his time at East Grinstead, in hospital and at the convalescent home at Saint Hill Manor, he now considers McIndoe to have been the 'finest psychologist he has ever met': 'We lived a fantasy life. It was as if the outside world didn't exist. We went out into the town but we were engrossed in our own world. It was group therapy. We considered ourselves bloody heroes.'

It was an immature way of life, but it was deliberately induced. Was it that to rebuild the Guinea Pigs they had to be taken back to adolescence and be made to grow up again as new people with new faces? 'Yes,' says Noel Newman, 'though I have my doubts about the psychological theorising.'

For three and a half years, the young doctor was on the receiving end of his profession. Like all the other Guinea Pigs he was encouraged to watch the Boss at work in the operating theatre, but in all that time he did not practise medicine. 'As a result,' he says, 'I became a better doctor.' He learned about pain. He developed patience and tolerance, and found out how a doctor should treat a patient. 'Patients should not be treated as half-wits, and no doctor should ever be too busy to answer the questions which a patient is worrying about.'

He also discovered what is meant by being cruel to be kind. To give his hands the chance to learn the skills of life again, he was made to use them, even when they hurt and even when they bled. He was given wool to thread and then tapestries to weave. 'We thought it sissy at the time but without it we would never have relearned the finer skills.'

But as skilful as he became with his newly formed hands, Noel Newman realised with regret that his ambitions to become a consultant surgeon would have to be abandoned. There was no question of him giving up medicine, but the avenues open to him were now limited. His mind turned to community medicine – public health as it was then called. He began to make enquiries, and spent a short trial period finding out about the discipline first hand. He liked what he saw, and in 1949 began a course in London which led to his taking his diploma in public health.

'It was very hard going back to school,' he recalls.

'Returning to a settled life and studying was very difficult after being with the boys.'

He would have preferred to have been involved in clinical medicine and not to have been training to become an administrator, but change his ideas he had to, following his accident. He came to terms with it. He worked first in Hove in Sussex, before moving to Bath in 1954 as deputy Medical Officer of Health. Although his responsibilities have changed, he has remained in the Bath area ever since. He and his wife Ruth live in a beautiful house just outside the city with a view which must match any in the county.

Today Noel Newman is semi-retired, working three days a week with children. 'In other words, I have extended my weekends.' His work with children involves both the routine and the specialised. Every child of school age in Britain receives a medical examination, a routine which has been responsible, in part, for the decline in many of the old illnesses which killed or crippled children at the turn of the century. The examination also spots children with sight or hearing problems. Many children have been given glasses for the first time as a result of having their eyes tested at school. In some cases, they have been able to see the school blackboard clearly for the first time, and the improvement in their school work has been quite noticeable.

Noel Newman's more specialised work is with handicapped children. He assesses their chances of being able to cope in ordinary schools, deciding if they need any specialised help at a special school, or even need the help of a home tutor.

Inevitably some of the children he examines notice that the doctor has got funny hands and holds things in a strange way. 'Most children say nothing; a few pass comment. If a child asks me what is wrong, I tell him. I say that I once had an accident. That is usually enough information to satisfy. Children don't want long explanations about the war. They only want to know so much. I answer the questions I am asked simply and fairly.'

Strangely, his own children did not notice their father's hands were different until they were quite old, perhaps ten. Or, at least, they said nothing.

Children, he feels, have far more tolerance and sympathy than adults. 'They will ask direct questions, but they don't mean to be unkind. They are very innocent. If I'm asked "why don't you have any hair?", I tell the child.'

Some adults, when presented with a damaged hand to shake, look askance. They shake the hand quickly as if it is something horrible, and quickly put their hand behind their back. The universal gesture of friendship and greeting is turned into an unwelcome ritual. But a child, if he sees Noel Newman's hand and notices its injuries, will hold it for a while and stroke it maybe. What an instinctive and unspoken rapport there is between a child – perhaps a handicapped one – innocently holding the hand of a disabled doctor. Nothing needs to be said. There is absolutely no embarrassment on either side.

Back in the adult world, the Guinea Pigs are facing the problems of old age. It is a strange thing but the Pigs with extensive skin grafts on the face do not appear to grow old. The grafts have a timeless, ageless quality to them. The tell-tale signs of advancing years – greying hair, broadening girth – are all there, but the face itself misleads the onlooker. Dr Newman is keenly aware of the problem of arthritis. Hands, he observes, will tend more to stiffness and pain as the years pass. In many cases Guinea Pigs have developed greater reliance on fewer joints than one would have expected if their hands had been complete. Consequently the overworked joints grow older quicker and the diseases of age catch up earlier.

Being a Guinea Pig has taught Noel Newman a great deal. It taught him how to come to terms with disappointment, when he realised he could no longer become a surgeon. It taught him about being a patient. 'I remember in my days as a medical officer of health seeing doctors discharging patients from hospital when they were medically fit enough to go home but when in all other ways they were not able to cope with the move. I could see clearly, having been a patient, that a woman who on discharge following an operation had to go back to a home with six children and a working husband, might, while well enough to leave hospital, not be strong enough to go back to her usual responsibilities.' In short, being a Guinea Pig taught Noel Newman how to be a better doctor.

Henry Standen

14

Henry Standen

The Guinea Pigs have all repaid their debts to the Queen Victoria Hospital and the Guinea Pig Club in their own way. One Pig became a plastic surgeon, many others devote their spare time and energies to helping others, especially the handicapped and disabled. Henry Standen must by now have repaid his debt to the hospital and the club a hundredfold.

With his wife Ann, he acts as unofficial liaison between his fellow club members, the hospital, and the town of East Grinstead. Henry is quiet and reflective: Ann is a bundle of energy. Between them they organise much of the Lost Weekend, are up to their ears in voluntary work at the hospital, and edit the Guinea Pig Club magazine.

Since coming under the care of Sir Archibald McIndoe and arriving at Ward Three, Henry has not moved far from 'the sty'. He met Ann at East Grinstead, on the top deck of a bus. She was a nurse, Henry a patient. After their marriage and after his discharge, they continued to live in the town. Henry commuted to London where he worked for a major oil company; Ann stayed in East Grinstead where she worked in the hotel and restaurant business.

Ann is a great organiser. Living in East Grinstead, it was inevitable she would take on a lot of the responsibility of arranging the annual reunion. At the end of every reunion 'she's exhausted – but very happy,' says Henry proudly. By October her energy returns and come November she is busy thinking about arrangements for ten months' time. Recently, she was given the nickname 'Scooter'. She was seen scooting here and there making sure that everything was in its place and there was a place for everything.

The Lost Weekend means a great deal to many dozens of Guinea Pigs. It gives them their boost of confidence for the year. It is important that each year it is the same, with the dance, the darts match, and the dinner, following the same regular pattern. But each year it has to be organised from scratch with nothing being left to chance. By ensuring the smooth running of the reunion, Ann and Henry Standen are contributing as much to the well-being of the Guinea Pigs today as McIndoe's treatment contributed in the past.

Henry had Guinea Piggery thrust upon him in December 1941. He was with 83 Squadron, in one of three aircraft with orders to mine the entrance to Brest harbour. It was a dangerous operation. The Hampdens had to fly low, in a straight line and very slowly to complete their mission. Henry was sure that it would be a one way trip. In the event, he had as close an encounter with death as is possible to have and still survive, but without the plane taking off.

As the aircraft in which he was navigator waited for take off, another plane tried to pass. What happened next is uncertain. Either the wings of the two aircraft touched, or they merely came close enough for a spark of static electricity to leap from one to another. Whatever the cause, Henry suddenly found the aircraft in which he was sitting was on fire. As the plane was laden with high explosives it was only a matter of time before an explosion. In desperation he managed to free his harness. He got free of the aircraft. There was an enormous explosion. He found himself lying flat on the runway. There was silence broken by the sound of debris falling from the air all around . . . .

For a number of weeks his life hung in the balance. They were weeks of strange memories and pain. Eventually he found himself at East Grinstead. By that time he was noticing things around him. 'The atmosphere of the place was different. It was so unlike a service hospital,'

Henry jokes, 'I thought I had been brought to a holiday camp by mistake.'

He quickly found himself swept into the spirit of the ward. He arrived at an ideal time. Guinea-Piggery was already established, the sherry party having taken place eight months or so before his arrival. At the same time, the Club still retained its pioneering vigour. McIndoe himself was much more in evidence at the hospital then than he was in the later years of the war, when illness kept him away from East Grinstead for long spells. Henry Standen remembers the Boss arriving in Ward Three on his days off wearing an old gardening jacket, and chatting to patients quite informally. Such sessions often ended up with McIndoe playing the grand piano in the ward to everyone's amusement. Later Henry was to realise that, relaxed as McIndoe might have appeared, he was in fact still working. He was monitoring the progress of his patients, seeing which ones were recovering their spirits, and which were in need of special care.

McIndoe was also using his spare time – or rather his time away from the operating theatre – to create the atmosphere in the ward which was an essential ingredient in his treatment of the Guinea Pigs. That special atmosphere has remained an essential part of the long-term treatment. It is an atmosphere which has to appear spontaneous but which has to be meticulously planned.

Today the planning often falls on the willing shoulders of Henry and Ann. In the same way that McIndoe assessed East Grinstead pubs and restaurants to find the ones most willing to take his Guinea Pigs, Henry and Ann finalise the arrangements for the Lost Weekend. It was originally held at the Whitehall in the centre of the town. It later moved to Ye Olde Felbridge to the north of East Grinstead. In 1978 the Guinea Pigs moved a few miles out of town, for the first time, to The Copthorne, an efficient hotel of high standard based around an old farm house. To accommodate the Guinea Pigs, a marquee was raised on the lawn. For the first time the club held its reunion under canvas.

The weekend followed its time-honoured pattern. On the afternoon of Friday 22 September, the Guinea Pigs and their wives began to converge on East Grinstead. Henry and Ann spent the afternoon in a whirl of activity. The first event, the dance, is traditionally open to the people of East Grinstead. Were any last-minute tickets needed? Where in the marquee would the band go, the tombola, the dance floor? As daylight faded and the Guinea Pigs who were staying at the Copthorne Hotel booked in, last-minute worries were still being ironed out. Some of the last-minute hitches were due to the fact that the club's activities were being filmed by Thames Television, but Henry and Ann took it all in their stride.

Later, in his capacity as editor of the club magazine, Henry was to describe the evening. It is typical of his modesty that he made no reference to his own part in making the evening a success.

As usual the music was by Peter Ricardo and his band, and things were much as before: good music, dancing and Cyril Jones, Bob Marchant and Ken Weller doing a roaring trade at the Tombola stall. At 10.30, David Lewin, the well-known show-business journalist, introduced Billy Marsh, the famous impresario who over the years has provided such outstanding cabaret artistes for us – all of whom have given their services without fees. Billy said what a great pleasure it was for him to help the club by doing this special job each year – and that this time the accent would be on nostalgia: Ann Shelton would sing some of the war-time favourites. Amid loud applause Ann appeared and captivated everybody. These old songs certainly brought back memories of the war years! The cameras filmed the singer and the audience, and at the end of the act there was what must be one of the most emotive moments in the Club's history. Jock Tosh, obviously a sick man, rose with difficulty and made an outstanding speech: direct, simple and straight from the heart. He thanked Ann for all the great pleasure she had given over the years but especially that night, and he presented her with a floral bouquet. Ann wept unashamedly and it is doubtful whether there was anyone who didn't have a lump in the throat. Ann Standen, who has been organising our dances for the past twenty seven years, said that she could not remember a time or occasion more touching.

Ann Shelton herself had sung to the Guinea Pigs once before. As a young girl, she had visited Ward Three. Her main memory of the visit being the strange, slightly sweet smell in the ward, a smell unlike that of a normal hospital. Later she realised that the smell was that of burned human tissue.

The Lost Weekend maintains an exhausting pace. The dance and other revelries continue until the wee small hours of Saturday. With age creeping up, fewer Guinea Pigs stay the course. Some come to a few events but not others. The hard core wake up late on Saturday morning, gulp a quick cup of strong black coffee and then set out for The Guinea Pig public house near the hospital.

The Guinea Pig pub was not built until after the war. It is a modern red-brick building designed to serve the new housing estate which backs on to the Queen Victoria Hospital. It was named The Guinea Pig as a tribute to the club. The first pint of beer was pulled at the bar by Sir Archibald himself.

Around the walls of the two bars there are dozens of pictures. Some of them are signed pictures of well-known personalities who have entertained the club members. There are pictures of various Pigs and a number of cartoons. The cartoons to look for are those signed H.S., the work of Henry Standen. Despite bad injuries to his hands, Henry has developed a considerable talent as a humorous artist. Like so many fellow Guinea Pigs, when Henry Standen decided to develop a skill, he did not aim at competence. He aimed at excellence.

He spent hour upon hour drawing. He learned again

how to hold a pen and pencil. He went up to London to
watch the master craftsman Leslie Illingworth at work.
Illingworth was at the time cartoonist of the *Daily Mail*
and a regular contributor to *Punch*. As he sat at his
drawing board in his office at the *Daily Mail*, he was full
of encouragement. 'You do it this way, mister,' he would
say in his gentle Welsh tones, explaining to Henry the
intricacies of cross-hatching and half-tone.

When he felt he was ready, Henry started submitting
his work to newspapers and magazines. He was to receive
the cartoonists highest accolade, acceptance by *Punch*.

As a direct result of his drawing ability, Henry was
asked by Blackie to take over the editorship of the Club
magazine. 'But I can't write,' Henry protested. 'Then fill
the pages with cartoons,' Blackie replied. Today, while
each edition of the magazine contains a handful of
Henry's sketches, his knowledge of layout and his writing
abilities have grown as well, to make the magazine
popular and essential reading for all Guinea Pigs and
their friends.

The magazine carries the bad news as well as the good.
In the New Year edition of 1979, Henry reported defeat
for the Club. At the annual darts match at The Guinea Pig
on the Saturday of the reunion weekend, the Club's team
was defeated for the fourth year running by a team from
the brewers.

Henry made no excuses. 'It's no use saying that the
brewer's men each have good hands and two eyes, whilst
the Guinea Pigs, some of them, have only one eye and a
shortage of fingers. Guinea Pigs are expected to rise above
that sort of trifling inconvenience.'

In an editorial, Henry wrote about the loss of the Sir
Max Aitken Darts Trophy: 'What can we do to stop the
rot? What ails our Guinea Pig arrowmen?' he wrote in
trenchant *Daily Express* style.

A number of suggestions were put forward – most of
them clearly facetious. One Guinea Pig suggested that the
Club put its team on a course of anabolic steroids; another
darkly suggested 'nobbling the opposition by putting a

Micky Finn in their beer'; somebody else muttered about getting in touch with the Mafia to ask a quotation for a Hit Man. . . .

'Tom Gleave thought we might follow the example of the British football clubs and buy in some new talent – "or maybe a team of native blowpipe darts flingers from Papua."

'All we can do is hope that next year the Guinea Pig team will go into serious training, will recover their skill and bring the trophy back again.'

One should not forget, reading a light-hearted account of a pub darts match, that the men involved have been disabled by war. In former generations, without the inspiration of the McIndoe team, they would have been pushed aside by society out of sight and out of mind. In a former age, many in society would have felt these men should have been hidden away, out of sight and mind.

From The Guinea Pig pub, it is a short walk to the hospital grounds. The Saturday afternoon of the Lost Weekend is a leisurely affair. There is a tea for all Pigs and their families. The annual general meeting of the Club is held; families and all non-Guinea-Pigs strictly excluded. Blackie and Russell Davies hold court, or rather make themselves available to individual Guinea Pigs with problems. A small office in the hospital is put aside and Blackie deals with general, social and financial queries, while Russell Davies listens to medical worries. As war memories fade, Guinea Pig problems do not. If anything they tend to grow. As one Pig was to put it at the dinner on Saturday evening, 'The chaps are beginning to show signs of wear and tear, old age, greying hair and the rest of it. . . . '

'I wouldn't put it quite like that,' said his companion. 'Let's say that you don't see many Guinea Pigs taking up this skate-boarding craze.'

The dinner is a strictly male occasion. Tables were laid out in the blue-and-white-striped marquee for the hundred and forty Guinea Pigs and their guests. Following tradition, three pictures were put on display: one of Sir Archibald McIndoe, one of Dr John Hunter and a third of Jill Mullens, the theatre sister. The guest of honour was the Lord Mayor of London, a man with a name as elaborate as the traditional dress of office; Air Commodore The Honourable Sir Peter Vanneck, G.B.E., C.B., A.F.C., A.E., M.A., D.L.

The dinner follows its time-worn path. It has its own rituals, the most entertaining being the singing of the Guinea Pig anthem, sung to the hymn tune 'The Church is one foundation', composed by Blackie to regularise a number of irreverent and inappropriate songs sung to the same tune many years ago.

> We are McIndoe's Army,
> We are his Guinea Pigs.
> With dermatomes and pedicles,
> Glass eyes, false teeth and wigs.
> And when we get our discharge
> We'll shout with all our might:
> 'Per adua ad astra',
> We'd rather drink than fight.
>
> John Hunter runs the gas works,
> Ross Tilley wields a knife.
> And if they are not careful
> They'll have your ruddy life.
> So Guinea Pigs, stand steady
> For all your surgeons' calls;
> And if their hands aren't steady
> They'll whip off both your ears.

The anthem, as it now stands, has plenty of opportunity for impromptu variation.

Speeches at the dinner are generally acknowledged to be of an unusually high standard. They are faithfully noted down by Henry Standen. In 1978, Guinea Pig Ian Craig took a few good-humoured jibes at the guest of honour. Reeling off his qualifications and honours, he said they left little of the alphabet unused. As a Scotsman, Ian Craig explained, he knew little about mayors. 'Where I come from we call them Provosts. And there is the story of

the English visitor to a Scots Burgh asking: "And do your
Provosts go about with a chain?" to get the reply: "Och,
no! We let them run about loose!" '

In recalling the Chief Guinea Pig's contribution to the
evening, Henry did not miss the high-light of his speech
when Tom Gleave let his notes stray too near the lighted
candle on his table. The notes began to singe and then
burst into flames. As he was quick to remark, one way to
cut a speech down to size.

Spontaneous combustion aside, Tom Gleave made a
special note of the innovatory spirit to be found in the club:

> I recently wandered through the Guinea Pig arch-
> ives and magazines, and what struck me forcibly
> was the atmosphere of innovation. Guinea Piggery
> provided the material for Archie, Percy Jayes, John
> Hunter, Russell Davies, George Morley and so on,
> the medical team, to innovate. But among the
> Guinea Pigs were great innovations in other fields. In
> 1941 there was the venerable Guinea Pig named
> Robert Atcherley, perhaps the greatest innovator
> among serving personnel in the RAF in the last war.
> His 'Drem' Lighting System was copied world-wide.

At the end of the dinner, husbands join wives again for
another party. It is known as Connie's party, not unnatur-
ally, as the hostess is Connie, Lady McIndoe. Connie is
both an attractive and formidable person. She was not at
Sir Archibald's side during the war years – they met and
married later – but she has adopted the Guinea Pigs with
great enthusiasm. She is a powerful ally to have when top
officials have to be tackled.

Even when the dinner and party are over, Henry and
Ann Standen are not able to relax completely. There is
Sunday's cocktail party to come, the occasion when
friends from the town and hospital meet the Guinea Pigs
around the swimming pool in the hospital grounds.

Inevitably as the years pass, the friends from the town
grow fewer in number. But the taxi driver who made a
special point of helping the Guinea Pigs still comes,

though he is in his nineties. There is the policeman who
turned an understanding blind eye to some of the Pigs in
more boisterous mood. Although retired, he still maintains an active interest in the life of the hospital, living
opposite the main entrance and manning the hospital
shop. Another guest at the party is Mabel Sailing, who as
a waitress at the Whitehall became a firm favourite with
many of the Guinea Pigs.

One close friend of the Club unable to come to any of
the events of the weekend last year was Bernard Arch.
Despite ill health, he managed to complete all the
paperwork for the weekend from his home. Bill Warman
collected the files from Bernard's Middlesex home and
took it to Henry and Ann for action. Bernard is the Club's
organising secretary. He is not a burned Guinea Pig, but
one of the Club's most trusted friends. A dispenser by
training, he came to East Grinstead in 1942 as a medical
clerk and became Blackie's assistant on the welfare side.

Henry Standen is now so involved in the Club that he
barely has time to think about his own disabilities. His
hands were badly damaged, but he uses them imagina-
tively and there are few things he cannot do. His main
worry is his eyes. A quarter of all Guinea Pigs have had
their sight impaired by war wounds. Henry needed new
eyelids. They provide very good, but not perfect protection for his delicate eyes. In total Henry underwent fifty
five operations. At one stage they came so thick and fast,
one every few weeks, that 'I thought no more of it than
going to have a haircut'. But in time he decided he had
had enough. 'You get to a pitch where you know you
could spend a lifetime getting improvements but you
decide to settle for what you've got.'

Henry's main worry in learning that he was to be
disfigured for life to some extent, however good the
surgery, was that he might not be presentable enough to
earn a living for himself. This worry in the end proved
groundless. He had no worries about attracting the attention of the young ladies of the day. Being a Guinea Pig
was glamorous. When he met Ann for the first time he

and a fellow Pig were in uniform and sitting upstairs in a
Green Line bus. They asked her to come and have a
drink. If they had not been Guinea Pigs she might have
hesitated; she did not normally go and drink with strange
young men on first meeting.

Today, as editor of the Club magazine, Henry is the
Club's postbox. He receives letters from around the world,
sometimes from Guinea Pigs who have been out of touch
for years. The magazine is produced twice a year and has
a distribution of eight hundred. Being editor is not just a
matter of sitting at home in East Grinstead collecting
foreign stamps. Henry is an experienced traveller. There
are both Australian and Canadian stamps in his passport
as a result of his visits to Guinea Pigs overseas. The
Canadian wing has occasional reunions, much on the lines
of the British reunion but not so often.

Henry epitomises the Guinea Pig spirit. He has risen
from the depths of hopelessness to live a full and active
life. But like so many Guinea Pigs, he does not live for
himself alone. He is quite selfless, in that he gives his time
and energies to others. He has learned the value of life.
He has learned it the hard way and has realised that it is
too precious a commodity to keep to himself.

Ross Tilley

15

The Overseas Guinea Pigs

Imagine not only being burned, having good looks and youth snatched away by fire and the use of hands and legs destroyed, but also imagine this trauma happening in a place far from home where all those around you are speaking in a language you barely understand. When this happened to Jimmy Wright in Italy he had hallucinations. He thought he was being tortured in a prisoner of war camp. In Bill Simpson's case, the experience sapped his belief in Britain and her ability to withstand the Nazi tide. But in the case of the Poles, Czechs, French and other Allied airmen who arrived at East Grinstead, Guinea Piggery came to the rescue. It crossed both language and cultural barriers.

There is a long list of Guinea Pigs with foreign sounding names, remarkable men like Capka, Glebocki, Krasnodebski, who left their own countries to fight for what they believed was right. The list of overseas Guinea Pigs contains some very English-sounding names as well; the Canadians, Americans and Australians, who, although speaking the same language as the English Guinea Pigs, must have found their ways and their habits as foreign as any.

The major overseas group, if only in size, is the Canadian group. In 1942, the Canadians were playing an increasing part in the war. They established a Canadian Plastic Surgery and Jaw Injuries unit at East Grinstead. Initially it consisted of five people. The surgeon, Squadron Leader Ross Tilley, and a staff of four. In June of that year a £20,000 grant was announced from the Canadian

Government for a new fifty-bed wing to be built at the hospital. It was to be used during the war for treating Canadian and Allied airmen and then to be handed over to the civilian authorities as a living memorial to the servicemen of Canada who had died and would die in action.

In these days of the National Health Service it is worth noting that thanks to the drive of McIndoe and the Canadians, the wing took only nine months to complete; less than three hundred days from inception to completion. The wing building finally marked the end of the era for the Queen Victoria Cottage Hospital and marked the beginning of one in which the hospital was to achieve international renown.

The name Canadian Wing now, however, has two meanings. As well as the physical premises at East Grinstead, there is also a Canadian Wing, or branch of the Guinea Pig Club. The president is Ross Tilley, who incidentally, by way of a souvenir of East Grinstead was presented with the air-raid siren which had been above his bedroom at his lodgings in the town, when the Canadians left the hospital in 1945. The Chief Canadian Guinea Pig was Bob Lloyd, now succeeded by Art Doyle. There are ninety or so members.

No visitor to Alberta in Canada should miss a visit to the Reynolds Automotive Museum. It is one of Alberta's showpieces. On display are old cars, tractors and commercial vehicles, indeed any kind of petrol or diesel driven transport. The man behind the enterprise is Guinea Pig Stan Reynolds, yet another Guinea Pig who kept up his interest in aviation and who started a small air taxi service, which grew into a very large enterprise.

Another Guinea Pig who maintains his interest in flying is Bill Anglin who lives in British Columbia. He has his own plane and flies fishing and hunting parties around British Columbia, the only way of transport in some of the more sparsely populated areas. The story is told of how on one trip, his passenger noticed his injuries and asked if he had been in the Air Force. When Bill said he had, the passenger quickly asked, 'Do you know Bob Lloyd?' Of course he did. 'Well,' said the passenger, 'I'm Bob Lloyd's boss.'

Bob Lloyd was the man responsible for reviving Guinea Piggery in Canada. It had survived unofficially until the early seventies, but then Guinea Pig Bob Lloyd decided it should be given a more official status. With the help of a kindly employer, who lent him secretarial assistance and office facilities, he set about contacting the trans-Atlantic Pigs and arranging a Canadian Lost Weekend.

Yet even without an official weekend, Guinea Pigs have a strange way of bumping into each other. Dr Ray Leupp, a rare teetotal Guinea Pig, is a vet from Ohio. He is also a keen horseman and on one occasion was crossing the border to Canada with his horse when he met the veterinary official at the border post. They noticed each other's injuries and a conversation began. 'Were you in the Air Force?' one asked. 'In Britain? Not at East Grinstead, surely?' The other vet turned out to be a fellow Guinea Pig, Dr Larry Somers.

One Guinea Pig who is unlikely to come across another Pig in such circumstances is George Wilson from Alberta. Given any opportunity he is to be found sailing the Pacific in his 32-foot sloop, *Mist Blew*. He has sailed from the American West Coast to Hawaii, overcoming natural hazards including hurricanes on the way.

Another get-away-from-it-all Guinea Pig is Tar Moore. For five or six months every year he becomes a backwoodsman. In a hut, at a remote spot called Goat Peak, he watches for forest fires. If he should see a 'smoke' he radios a warning to the fire services. He spends his time reading and writing and watching the wildlife.

A Guinea Pig who is very much a city-dweller is Hank Ernst of Calgary. He left his job with Air Canada, in the air freight section, and has set up a busy second-hand-car business.

One Pig, who perhaps had less time for the English than any during his stay at the Sty, is now one of the few to have settled in England to live. Gerry Dufort, a French

Canadian was a wireless operator in the Stirling piloted by
Bertram Owen Smith. In his time at East Grinstead he
made it quite clear that he thought the English a strange
sort of people and was the originator of a number of most
unflattering wisecracks. He went back to Canada to live
after the war, but his attitude to the English must have
been softening, as eventually he was to come back to
settle.

In keeping with the Guinea Pigs' tradition for black and
uncomplimentary humour, the Club's anthem pays tribute
to the overseas members.

> We've had some mad Australians,
> Some French, some Czechs, some Poles,
> We've even had some Yankees,
> God bless their precious souls.
> While as for the Canadians,
> Ah! That's a different thing,
> They couldn't stand our accent,
> And built a separate wing.

The mad Australians are perhaps less organised than the
Canadians today, but Guinea Piggery still flourishes
Down Under. Amongst the characters are two friends,
Freeman Strickland and Ken Gilkes.

'Strick' from Melbourne met Gilkes from Sydney in
1943 at East Grinstead. They teamed up immediately and
their respective families are now very close. They both
had a rough time. Strick, now a businessman with a
shipping agency, crashed in a Spitfire in Italy. He was
rescued by a local peasant and taken to a monastery. He
was assumed missing until discovered by chance by an
Irish priest. Gilkes and he met up in the ward and Strick,
through his constant encouragement, helped save his new
friend's life after a particularly difficult operation.

Gilkes and Strick, however, became famous for their
prowess as souvenir hunters. It is part of the Club's
mythology that when they returned to Australia they both
had to pay a fortune in excess luggage charges, they had
so many mementos packed away. The story is also told of

their visit to East Grinstead for a Lost Weekend in the 1950s. They slipped away from the dinner during the speeches and nicked a lobster pot sign from the bar at Ye Olde Felbridge Hotel and took it back to McIndoe's house where they exhibited it.

George Taylor is a Guinea Pig with a liking for practical jokes of a less active kind. He was at Sydney University and one day spotted some workmen erecting barriers in the street to dig up the road. He telephoned the police and tipped them off that a group of students were about to disrupt traffic by the university by dressing up as council workmen and digging a hole in the road. He then telephoned the council to warn them that a group of students, dressed as policemen, were about to descend on their work party to arrest them for unlawfully digging holes in the highway. George Taylor, it is reported, watched the ensuing battle with great amusement.

The story of the overseas Guinea Pigs is studded with courage. They suffered as much as their English counterparts, perhaps more, in that they could never have family and friends to visit them.

One foreign Guinea Pig, however, had a visit of a very unwelcome and sinister kind. Raz, or Rasumov to give the full name of the only Russian Guinea Pig, was found badly burned in Germany and brought to East Grinstead for treatment. He was given honorary rank as a British officer and he joined the Guinea Pigs in their social life and in the ward. One day he was seen talking to some strangers near the hospital grounds. A few hours later he was reported missing. The Russian Embassy was contacted. Officials there were polite but unhelpful. No trace of Raz has ever been found. It is assumed by the Club that he was 'persuaded or taken back to the Soviet Union or disposed of'. Inquiries continued for many years until it was felt that, if he were still alive in Russia, it would do more harm than good to try to contact him. The Guinea Pig File on Honorary Flight Lieutenant V. Rasumov was reluctantly closed.

One foreign Guinea Pig who has no difficulty in

returning to East Grinstead is the only Turkish member of the Club, Kemal Intepe. He is a regular attender at the Lost Weekend and comes to the town a number of weeks in advance. He parks his estate car, which serves as his temporary home, in the hospital grounds and offers his services to the hospital in an entirely voluntary capacity. He reached the rank of colonel in the Turkish Air Force but is more than willing to help out as a porter, cleaner or ward orderly at the Queen Victoria Hospital. In his halting English he explains to anyone who asks that it is the least he can do to repay the hospital and the country which restored him to health, after an accident in which every bone in his face was smashed.

While East Grinstead as a town and a number of other places in the South East of England grew used to seeing wounded servicemen around, it was to come as quite a shock to many places overseas when the Guinea Pigs returned home. To prepare the Canadians for the blow a film was produced, a documentary about an imaginary Canadian airman who was given plastic surgery. The star of the film was not a Canadian but an Englishman, Jack Allaway. Allaway was always considered by McIndoe to be his star patient, and it would be hard to disagree. He was given a Canadian uniform and the filming began. The film *New Faces for Old* proved a great success not only in preparing the way for the returning Canadians but also in giving Jack Allaway, the star, a new confidence in life.

There were over one hundred and seventy overseas Guinea Pigs, more than a quarter of the total number. Some have lost contact with the Club but, where contact has been maintained, it is easy to see the overseas Guinea Pigs and their British counterparts have a great deal in common. They have shared the same experiences and the same treatment. They have shared the inspiration of McIndoe and been given the will to carry on living life to the full despite disfigurement and disability. A large number have proved to be very successful in their jobs and professions. There are top grade academics and successful businessmen, including a millionaire or two, among the members on the other side of the Atlantic. But it is also true to say that many of the overseas Guinea Pigs will suffer the same problems as the British Guinea Pigs in years to come. They, too, are determined to overcome them. Guinea Piggery transcends geographical, national, cultural and language barriers.

16

Plastic Surgery

Most advances in plastic surgery have had cruel and barbarous beginnings. It took the purposeless slaughter of the First World War for the pedicle method of transferring skin from one part of the body to another to be perfected by McIndoe's early mentor, Sir Harold Gillies. It took the madness of Hitler and the horrific burns produced by the Second World War to spur on the genius of Sir Archibald McIndoe himself. Yet fifteen hundred years ago, on the Indian sub-continent, the rhinoplasty technique for reconstructing the nose was devised to right the wrongs produced by a particularly nasty custom.

A Hindu woman of the time caught with a lover by her husband or father had her nose severed from the face. It was the right of an aggrieved male to mutilate a woman in this way, even on suspicion. However, mistakes were made. A wrongly accused wife could often be marked for life as an adulteress. As necessity is the mother of invention, the medical men of the day devised a way of building a new nose. The method they used is still the basis of today's. Chief Guinea Pig Tom Gleave sports a McIndoe nose very similar to the one produced by the age-old Indian method as described during the eighteenth century in the *Madras Gazette.*

Plastic surgery is not new. The father of European plastic surgery lived in Shakespeare's day in Italy. He was a professor at Bologna, Gaspare Tagliacozzi. Shortly before his death he published a textbook of plastic surgery describing how to raise a flap of skin from the arm, with which to rebuild the nose or ear. It must have taken great courage on the patient's part to submit to such an operation. Not only were there no anaesthetics but also Tagliacozzi insisted the patient be kept in a rigid harness, akin to a straight-jacket, for forty days after the operation.

It is true that in the pre-anaesthesia days, surgeons were men who worked at great speed, but plastic surgery being such a delicate art always took time. In the early nineteenth century the British surgeon, Carpue, took fifteen minutes to perform a rhinoplasty compared with one and a half hours today. As one leading surgeon of the day was able to amputate a leg in twenty-five seconds, rhinoplasty must have seemed to the patient to have been an agonising eternity. Incidentally the same high speed surgeon once took away three of his assistant's fingers by accident, such was his haste to take off a patient's leg.

Along with all branches of surgery, plastic surgery made its greatest strides as a result of the twin nineteenth-century developments: anaesthesia and antiseptics. The notion that surgical implements, operating theatres and surgeon's hands had to be clean, has saved thousands of lives.

With or without anaesthetics, the nineteenth century was a creative period in plastic surgery. The cleft-palate and hare-lip operation became well established. The rhinoplasty was refined. The skin taken from the forehead by the Indian method and twisted down to form a new nose often suffered through lack of blood. Twisting the skin constricted the blood supply. The French surgeon, Lisfranc, suggested the refinement of taking the skin at a 45° angle to the line of the nose thus producing less strain on the blood vessels.

The modern plastic surgeon's vocabulary pays tribute to his nineteenth-century forebears. The Ollier-Thiersch graft, one of thin skin, is called after two pioneers, as is the Wolfe-Krause graft. This is a thick graft of skin which is used as a free graft, called after the Scottish surgeon who pioneered the work and the German who refined it. The cutting of such grafts has been the subject of continued refinement. A museum case at the Queen.Victoria Hospital shows the various surgical instruments used, all bar one exhibit which has been 'borrowed' as it has a modern use – slicing smoked salmon. One of the greatest breakthroughs in cutting skin grafts of a uniform thickness came in the 1930s with the invention of the dermatome by the American surgeon Earl C. Padgett.

In September 1939, when Archibald McIndoe arrived at Queen Victoria Hospital, the pattern of plastic surgery was established. It was a branch of surgery with three strands. First the treatment of injury, specialising in burns; secondly the repair of congenital deformities, and thirdly there was, and is, the controversial cosmetic strand.

The treatment of injury had been static since the First World War, when plastic surgery had made such advances that it had become the main branch of military surgery. It was the first strand to which McIndoe put his mind as consultant plastic surgeon to the RAF. For the first months of the war, the phoney war, he had little to do but plan. From September 1939 until the end of the year he had only 74 service cases to deal with in the 146 bed hospital. The next year was to see over 700 Service patients being admitted to the cottage hospital and almost as many local patients.

The Battle of Britain provided the first severely burned victims of war; Hurricane and Spitfire burns – skin and flesh roasted for a brief second by an intense blast of heat. McIndoe was to build up such a bank of experience in dealing with these burns that on meeting a patient for the first time he was able to amaze him with a Sherlock Holmes act. 'I see you were in a Spitfire, but why weren't you wearing your gloves, you clot? You had your goggles on though and your helmet – but it wasn't buttoned up was it?' If you knew the tell-tale signs, McIndoe's observations were really quite elementary. Because Battle of Britain burns, however intense, were short-lived, clothing offered good protection. The burned face of an airman, for example, who had been wearing goggles had the outline of the goggles etched into the flesh and on the inside of the scar-line the skin and eyes were almost unscathed.

The textbook treatment of burns was considered by McIndoe to be primitive. It involved the application of tannic acid and gentian violet which healed the skin in a most unsightly manner and caused damage to more delicate areas, especially eyelids. If McIndoe made one major breakthrough in burns treatment, it was to convince the medical profession and military authorities to replace their standard treatment with the saline bath. He firmly believed that the plastic surgeon was in the front line in tackling burns and was not there just to be called upon to cover or remove ugly scars after tissue had healed.

Incidentally, it is part of Guinea Pig folklore that McIndoe invented the Heath Robinson-style saline bath after watching the progress made by burned airmen who had fallen in the sea. They did so much better, it is said, than those who came to earth on dry land. Medically, however, this is unlikely. The saline bath, to be of value, had to be kept at blood heat, a lot warmer than the English Channel, and the salinity of the water had to be kept at a constant level which does not naturally occur in the waters around Europe.

Nearly forty years on, perhaps inevitably, the saline bath treatment itself is being questioned. It is not being suggested it was harmful, just that the best thing to use to cover burned skin is now considered to be skin itself. It is interesting to note that McIndoe in 1940 was advocating precisely the same approach, but at that time there were a number of drawbacks, drawbacks which have still not been entirely overcome. There is no doubt that the best protection for exposed tissue is skin. This is the principle behind the Gillies tube pedicle; if a flap of skin has to be raised and the risk of infection is to be minimised, the flap can be turned in on itself – with nature's tissue protector, skin, on the outside. It cannot, however, be any skin. As in all transplant surgery there is the rejection problem.

The father of plastic surgery, Tagliacozzi, failed to recognise the rejection difficulty and in the nineteenth

century an attempt was made to cover burns on one
patient with a sheep's skin. Not quite such a mad idea as it
might seem, though perhaps a little cruel. An old print
exists showing the patient lying on a bed with the live
sheep strapped in a cage next to her. A broad flap of skin
had been cut from the sheep and had been stretched
across the patient's back. The records of the day show that
both patient and sheep survived. The skin provided a
useful temporary cover and foreshadows one modern
technique, the use of areas of pig skin as a human skin
substitute for short-term protection.

The advances in burns treatment during the Second
World War were also linked with advances in the treatment of shock, post-operative infection and anaesthesia.

Dr John Hunter, McIndoe's anaesthetist, was a man
open to new ideas. Admittedly in his personal habits he
tended to be outlandish. He far preferred to slip a white
coat over his civilian clothes when getting down to work
and spurned full theatre garb. Cap and mask were
anathema. But in his work he was imaginative as well as
jolly and humane in his approach. 'Just a little prick, if
you'll excuse the expression,' was his catch phrase as he
injected a Guinea Pig just before going on the 'slab'.

Between them, McIndoe and Hunter made giant strides
in establishing a new relationship between surgeon and
anaesthetist. Russell Davies describes the development in
this way.

> The visit of the surgeon with, for example, his
> registrar, house surgeon and ward sister is so often a
> little awe-inspiring, and questions which the patient
> would like to ask are, in this atmosphere, frequently
> forgotten – or, if remembered, suppressed. After the
> patient has recovered from this visitation and has
> had time to reflect, along comes the anaesthetist on
> his own, and whose conversation is wholly compre-
> hensible, dwelling as it does on smoking and drink-
> ing habits, ability to exercise and so forth. Against
> this less formal background, the patient may well

recover his composure and his memory and pose the questions not already posed to the surgeon. These the anaesthetist should be able to answer and, in due course, add to the information already secured by the surgeon. This information may be medical – or social. What are the prospects of a full return to work? Will earning capacity be unaffected or even improved by the proposed surgery? Will family life be affected? And so forth. So the day has now departed, hopefully for ever, where the anaesthetist is a mere technician who has no contact with the patient, but is someone who can also play a fundamental role in achieving McIndoe's objective of fully functional return to the community.

The Second World War gave the Queen Victoria Hospital its great reputation. It dropped the word cottage in its title and became the country's, if not the world's leading hospital in its speciality. With the building of the Canadian Wing the hospital had 230 beds. McIndoe, being a persuasive and irresistible character, cajoled wealthy individuals, with whom he mixed freely, and generous organisations to give the hospital money. The money poured in. Hundreds of individuals gave lesser sums, through the Peanut Club and other voluntary bodies. At one stage so much money was pouring into the hospital, in those pre-National Health days, that the local press were asked to assure the citizens of East Grinstead that their own contributions were still needed. By way of an interesting aside, in 1944 it cost £6 4s 11d to keep a patient at the hospital every week.

Perhaps McIndoe's greatest achievement in the field of plastic surgery was to lend the respectability of the first strand of plastic surgery to the third strand, cosmetic surgery. To quote a number of Guinea Pigs, 'McIndoe as well as being a great surgeon was a great psychologist'; he recognised the mental damage which severe injury could cause, especially when the victims were virile and handsome young men. He was as much concerned with

pushing his patients out into society as in reconstructing
their injured hands and faces, often being cruel to be kind.
Russell Davies recalls one case.

> I remember one dynamic young man, most despera-
> tely burnt, whom I asked local Guinea Pigs to visit
> while he was in hospital. This they did, and in due
> course I asked them to act as his companions when
> he first ventured outside the hospital grounds. So,
> one evening, four scarred 'Pigs' collected the healing
> patient, put him in a car, and drove off to the local.
> On arrival, they hopped out, leaving the patient in
> the car. The next morning, when I asked him how he
> had got on, he told me what had happened – and
> added what a rotten lot he at first thought they were,
> then added 'But I thought "Well! if they can do it, I
> can too".' And he in turn climbed out of the car and
> entered the pub. Never again was that man afraid of
> entering society.

McIndoe's programme of treatment was a two-pronged
attack. He would, on the one hand, reconstruct a patient
physically. The process was slow, with each operation
producing a marginal improvement. On the other hand he
was preparing the patient for a life in which some degree
of disability or disfigurement was an inescapable fact. The
treatment finished when the patient himself decided that
he was happy to try to cope with life with what he
had – again a common Guinea Pig quote: 'You get to a
stage, perhaps after ten, twenty or thirty operations, when
you decide the next operation isn't worth it. You've had
enough. You can live with the face you've got.'

One of today's plastic surgeons, John Bennett of East
Grinstead, prefers to think of plastic surgery as the
surgical branch of psychiatry. If there is a patient with a
psychiatric problem, instead of giving him a pill it is
sometimes possible to operate.

He tells the story of one patient, a woman of thirty-two
who looked like a woman of over fifty. Her skin had

sagged and prematurely aged as a result of radio-therapy she had been given for a skin complaint. She was acutely depressed by her condition. All the life in her marriage had drained away. Her social life was non-existent. When John Bennett met her he felt that her life could even end tragically in suicide. He decided to give her a face-lift. There was no way she could afford to pay for such a 'cosmetic' operation, but the surgeon decided it was so important for her mental welfare, even to save her life, that he decided to treat her on the National Health. Some of his colleagues were horrified but Bennett's decision was vindicated by the woman's recovery, her return to normal life and the saving of her marriage.

Not every case is as clear cut. There are patients who seek cosmetic operations and have to be told in no uncertain terms that an operation is unnecessary. All operations carry an element of risk to the patient. No surgeon can ignore the remote possibility of a cardiac arrest on the operating table. No operation is guaranteed. Face-lifts can go wrong. Many reputable plastic surgeons have had to repair the damage caused by the less scrupulous fringe members of the profession.

One of Mr Bennett's first duties on arriving at East Grinstead was to tell an ageing homosexual who was demanding a second face-lift that he had no intention of operating. He remembers also two wealthy continental girls asking for an operation to alter the shape of their eyes. 'We had our noses done last year and thought we'd have our eyes done this year.' They too were sent packing. 'I do not operate on complete, healthy people,' John Bennett was to tell them.

In all probability, the two girls took the next plane to Casablanca. There they would have had no problem in finding a willing commercial clinic. Money to them was no object, and judging from the opportunities which exist for plastic surgeons to make their fortune on the fringes of medical practice, it would not have been difficult to find a surgeon.

There are no reference books, no rules of thumb to

guide the plastic surgeon when presented with a patient asking for cosmetic surgery. Indeed there are no hard and fast rules for him to follow in treating burns. McIndoe himself loved to work in a turmoil. The back-up services from theatre staff to medical photographers had to retain a semblance of order, but the surgeon worked hard and long, switching approach and attack to suit every patient individually. Like a chess grandmaster McIndoe would operate on a patient with the fifth or sixth operation or move ahead in mind, but could always switch back quickly if the need arose.

Today plastic surgeons still have to treat each patient as an individual. One patient with an unsightly feature could well be right when he blames it for holding him back at work. When operated on and the feature corrected, all his troubles could be at an end. Another patient with the same problem could have the same operation and yet find no improvement in his life. He might turn on the surgeon and blame him for having 'ruined his life', transferring the blame for his own inadequacies from himself to an outsider.

The plastic surgeon must be aware of this danger. Patients may ₁sometimes attempt legal action or even threaten violence. But their difficulties should not be exaggerated. The need for a branch of surgery to reconstruct the human body is undeniable. The first time I visited the Queen Victoria Hospital was about seven years ago when I drove a friend and her baby son there. He had been born with a hare lip and cleft palate. He had all the usual feeding problems associated with the deformity and, if he had been allowed to grow up with his mouth unrepaired, would have led a miserable stigmatised life. The little boy was successfully operated on and will grow up with just the thinnest of scars on his top lip. Few people will give it a second thought. There are other congenital deformities which can be tackled successfully. Some babies are born with a web of skin between the fingers. Some children have protruding ears which lead to a miserable life at school.

Other deformities and injuries result from accidents; on the roads, at work or in the home. Not all injuries can be mended completely. At any given time there will be a patient at East Grinstead who, once the surgical treatment is complete, will still be disfigured and will have to leave the ward and go out and learn how to face society again.

Today, however, these patients will not have the spirit of Guinea Piggery to sustain them. The patients are no longer a homogeneous group. With the exception of firemen burned in the course of duty, burns patients in particular are not mainly healthy youngsters who have been suddenly disabled. They tend to be the disadvantaged or vulnerable whose burns and scars compound an existing inadequacy or helplessness. The McIndoe burns unit is occupied mostly by children, the very old or the mentally unstable. It is a difficult place for the nursing staff to work in. There is little chance to talk with patients. If they are physically able to talk they are often too inarticulate or withdrawn to converse.

The burns unit tackles the old killers with great success. Fewer people today, if they survive a burn will die from shock, dehydration, infection or the metabolic changes which can reduce a healthy man to almost half his weight. With the availability of plasma, artificial feeding and antibiotics, more patients survive the early traumatic weeks than would have done in McIndoe's day.

The full recovery of many of the patients will depend as much on the care and experience of families, welfare workers and psychiatrists as on the skill of the surgeon. The surgeon's contribution will depend on his being able to reconstruct a patient as completely and as quickly as possible; being able to graft skin which takes immediately and does not differ in colour from the skin around, making it obvious that a graft has been made; and being able to complete the whole procedure in as few stages as possible. Some of the Guinea Pigs had eighty operations, a total unlikely to be topped by a modern patient with similar injuries.

But will surgeons ever be able to produce perfect grafts

or reconstruct damaged hands which not only work efficiently but look perfect as well? In theory, yes, but only if the problems of tissue rejection are solved and the rapid progress in micro-vascular surgery is maintained. In micro-vascular surgery the surgeon can join small blood vessels and the other minute components of human tissue. Photographs in the medical library at East Grinstead show fingers and hands, even whole limbs, which have been accidentally severed from the body and then rejoined. The more refined and detailed the surgery, the greater the use which returns to the severed part. There have been operations in which the surgeon has amputated a toe and raised it to the hand to replace a missing thumb. Hip bone, surrounding tissue and skin can be raised to replace a jaw and injured face.

Such procedures, as with any graft, always rob Peter to pay Paul. They involve taking a less essential part of the body to replace a more essential part. Think what the advantages would be if grafts could be transferred from one person to another, in the same way that a kidney can be transferred. People who now carry a kidney donor card, saying that they would be willing to give their kidney to save a life in the event of their own death, could carry a general donor's card.

Is this too far fetched? John Bennett thinks not. Sooner or later someone will find the solution to the rejection problem and a whole new era in plastic surgery will open up.

Will the breakthrough come about as a result of research being carried out at East Grinstead? It is a possibility. The hospital is certainly to the fore in the development of micro-vascular surgery. The giant strides forward made by the hospital during the Second World War gave it pre-eminence in its field. If it can make the next great advance, the hospital will keep its position. To do this the Queen Victoria Hospital might have to give a new impetus to its research and teaching roles. One thing is certain: the hospital of McIndoe and his team will not rest on its laurels.

17

The Future

The Guinea Pig Club has faced many crises in its history. Most of them, it has overcome. But, nearly forty years after it was formed, it faced a problem as perplexing as any since its inception. Put quite simply: how is the Club going to face the future?

Uncharacteristically, the Club is unsure about the solution to the problem. No one doubts the members' motives to continue caring for their fellow men, yet there are so many cross-currents obscuring the issue, so many emotional eddies pulling the Guinea Pigs this way and that. It was Geoffrey Page who found the right words to summarise the problem: 'We are reaching the stage', he said, at the Club's 1978 annual meeting, 'when, like the elderly reader of *The Times*, we turn to the Obituary columns every morning, and, if our name's not in it, we decide to get up and shave, ready to face the new day . . . .'

The annual meeting is as well-attended as any function during the Guinea Pig weekend at East Grinstead. It precedes the annual dinner on the Saturday. It was a sunny September afternoon; the Guinea Pigs were in their shirt-sleeves, or light sweaters, or blazers and flannels. It was a cheerful business meeting. Looking along the rows of faces, so many of them bearing the marks of a score of operations, the grafted skin that will never wrinkle, could not conceal the fact that this is an ageing Club. As the members age, so their physical and psychological problems will grow. At the same time, those men without whom the Club would not properly function,

Edward Blacksell

such as Russell Davies and Blackie, Gleave and Arch, Standen, Gallop and the rest of the committee, are also getting older. So who is going to replace them? Who is going to join the Club that hasn't had a new member for more than thirty years? Or is the Guinea Pig Club simply going to fade away, with, as Geoffrey Page puts it, the final annual meeting taking place between 'the last two survivors, each in a bathchair'?

The dilemma is real and understandable. To accept new members the Club must, of necessity, alter the rules. And those rules are both a tradition and a protection, a link with the Club's beginnings when the objectives and the parameters were pledged over a glass of sherry, an insurance against infiltration by those who haven't precisely shared the experiences and the needs of this extraordinary group of men.

There is a clear majority that resists change. Their view is that many clubs exist to help many people, and that they, as the Guinea Pig Club, are only too willing to visit hospitals and work for charity, in order to pass on what they've learned. However, that should be as far as it goes, because what makes the Guinea Pig Club unique is the harrowing experience in a wartime context that every member has endured. And the Club's specific aim has always been to soften the impact of that experience and hasten the recovery from it.

It is a difficult argument to resist. But it sidesteps one question: are the current members content that the lessons they have learned, in facing both the world and themselves, should die with them?

Goodwood, 1966, the Easter motor-racing meeting: the stands are packed, the colours bright, the noise deafening. Peter Procter, Yorkshire businessman and one of Britain's most promising drivers, has made an excellent start to the new season. It is his sixth race of the year, this time a saloon car event.

The first lap sorts out the fast from the not-so-fast. The drivers jockey for position. The bend is a tight, right-hander.

It's called St Mary's. There is a bunch of twenty-five or
thirty cars. It appears so well ordered. Then, the pattern
changes. One car appears to take off. It turns over in
mid-air. The picture is both gripping and obscene. The
car is Peter Procter's . . . .

> You're ready for it, and yet, you're unprepared. I
> knew what had happened. Someone had shunted
> into my rear and the petrol tank had exploded. But
> the main thing in my mind was simply to get out. I
> mean, the whole thing had blown up and I was still
> inside. I was strapped in the car, fortunately, and as
> soon as it stopped rolling over, I undid the seat-
> straps. At least, I tried to, and then, because I was
> virtually upside down, I fell into a heap in the corner
> of the car.
>
> I knew I had problems and that the car was on fire.
> I knew, instinctively, that I had to try to cover my
> face with my hands to protect it from the flames. But
> I needed my hands to get out, as well. And I couldn't
> see with my hands covering my face. It was a puzzle.
> It was like trying to get out in the dark.
>
> I eventually struggled out through the side window
> on the driver's side. It seemed to be all over in a
> matter of seconds. In fact, I suppose it took about
> half a minute.
>
> There was no feeling of panic at all, which is
> surprising. I just knew I had to get out. It was just
> something I had to do.
>
> And, as I lay there on the ground, I didn't feel any
> great pain at all. The marshals came and covered me
> with coats and things and I was grateful that I didn't
> lose consciousness. You worry about odd things. Two
> of the marshals who cared for me, came to see me in
> hospital afterwards and I assumed I might have
> sworn at them. I wanted to apologise to them, but I
> was pleased to discover that I'd behaved like a
> gentleman, they said. In fact, one of them told me I'd
> requested, quite politely: 'Excuse me, would you

mind telephoning for an ambulance.' Which, on reflection, is a funny thing to say, isn't it?

Peter Procter's hands, face and body were pitifully burned. His experience is one that every Guinea Pig will recognise. And Peter Procter knows the Guinea Pigs well, because they helped him when he needed it . . . . He was in hospital for seven months. There was reconstructive surgery to be carried out, he'd completely lost his eyelids, for instance, surgery that was still going on twelve years later. And there was the heart-searching self-examination to be endured.

I wondered how I'd cope. You see, I considered it was a self-inflicted injury. I'd put my life at risk, and brought anguish to my family, wilfully if you like. I'd always driven, knowing there was a certain amount of family opposition and, in the most private moments, I suppose I was determined now not to let anyone see that it was getting me down. I had to put a brave face on things, for the sake of my own pride, as much as to protect others . . . .

But I honestly didn't know how I'd cope when I left hospital. My wife was a great comfort to me. And I'll never forget what my eldest son said, very early on. He was just twelve then, and he came in to visit me and I said to him, almost by way of an apology, 'Well, Derek, I've made a mess of it this time.'

And he said, quite spontaneously, 'Never mind, Dad. You're still the same Dad underneath.'

And then my friends, my good friends, stuck by me very close at the time. A number of motor racing people came to visit me. Graham Hill, in particular, flew down several times to see me. He was a good man. So psychologically I knew I wasn't being thrown on the scrapheap. But, however good and kind anyone was, they couldn't tell me what lay ahead, because they'd never travelled that road.

The turning point, for Peter Procter, was a series of visits from members of the Guinea Pig Club.

> They'd heard I was in hospital and they wanted to
> help. And I suppose my first view of them was really
> the first close view I'd ever had of someone really
> badly burned; certainly, they were the first badly
> burned people I ever got to know well.
>
> Many of them were much worse than I thought I
> was going to be. And they were obviously coping
> with life so well. They came in and cheered me up.
> And they gave me encouragement and comfort, and
> the knowledge, without actually saying it, that they'd
> done it all, seen it all, been through it all, already.
> And if they could do it, so could I. If I had any
> doubts before I came to know them, I didn't after-
> wards.

Peter Procter, as has already been said, knows the Guinea
Pigs well. They're his friends. But he's not one of them.
He has attended the Lost Weekend, as have a few other
privileged individuals, and has been welcome, only as a
guest.

Yet Peter Procter can help others, just as the Guinea
Pigs have helped him. And he's anxious to do so. If
Procter is so willing, what of other young people who have
endured the experience of burning and survival? He
hesitates to intrude into what is, after all, a family debate.
But his views are too important to ignore. Problems seen
from another angle sometimes seem less awesome.

> I'm firmly convinced that the Club has a lot to
> contribute. They've helped me, they've helped a lot
> of people. It would be a shame to let the Club die
> out. On the other hand, I can understand the feelings
> of many of them, that this is a special Club, a unique
> Club.
>
> But, if the alternative is to let the Club die, surely
> some formula like associate membership, or some
> other form of words, might be considered? You see,
> *because* it's so special, the Club almost has a duty to

carry on. To go on spreading the word that it is possible to survive, to those who've been burned in a rather less glamorous way than in a crashing aircraft or an exploding fighter plane. Those people, people leading unexciting lives, often don't know how to handle the shock of it all. They tend to become hermits, to hide from life.

And the more often they can be told, 'Now look, beauty's only skin deep', the better. I mean, that's been my experience. Life is still the same to me, looking out. In fact, it's better, in many cases.

That's what the Guinea Pigs helped to teach me. And that's why the Club's worth fighting for, because these men have already helped hundreds of people who otherwise would have thrown in the towel. It would be a great shame if all that stopped, wouldn't it?

None of this was said at the 1978 annual meeting of the Guinea Pig Club. After Geoffrey Page had said his piece, his sentiments were noted and it was decided to take no further action. As Tom Gleave said afterwards: 'There's no panic. We're busy spreading the word. There's plenty of time. . . . '

How the Guinea Pig Club will solve the problem isn't clear. That they *will* solve it, without acrimony, is more certain. For the success of the Club is built on the ability to create and understand relationships. It's been that way from the beginning. Russell Davies remembers the lessons that had to be learned then:

We had to grope towards an understanding of the many relationships: the surgeon with the patient, the patient with the surgeon (another thing altogether), the surgeon with the anaesthetist, the nurse, and above all, with society itself. The spur to the examination - or a re-examination of these relationships - was probably the fact that virtually all the patients were committed to a long stay in hospital of, as it proved, up to four years or even beyond. Not infrequently this stay involved a total of ten, twenty, thirty, or even more operations. Under these circum-stances the somewhat traditional relationship and reserves of the surgeon patient relationship just could not be maintained. The patient just had to be made aware of the surgical plans which had been made for him. How these were to be staged and their degree of failure and success. And as a quite logical consequence of this, how he was ultimately to be rehabilitated, both medically and socially.

So the processes of information were begun – this in the early 1940s. It is interesting that nowadays we hear repeatedly that this process of information should take place, in the 1970s. An idea proven in the 1940s has still to reach full flowering in the 1970s.

This process of communication was energy-demand-ing, time-consuming and unconventional. But no patient's question was ever turned aside . . . .

So the die was cast in those early days. The question, which now cannot be left unanswered, is being posed to the Club itself. What is your own view of your future job in society; what more will you, as a Club, contribute?

The words of Russell Davies come from a lecture he gave to the British Association of Plastic Surgeons in December 1976. It was the ninth annual McIndoe Memorial Lecture and, inevitably, Dr Davies talked of 'The Boss', a man, he said, 'who began the activity of building bridges between the patients and society and who continued that activity vigorously until his death'. Invari-ably, McIndoe succeeded and it is worth quoting Davies again, for few knew him better, on the reasons why he was successful:

I believe that McIndoe's greatest quality was that of courage. And it was displayed over so many years and in so many ways. The fact that he left the assured success of the Mayo Clinic as and when he did displayed courage. The fact that he successfully went against the trends of the times and refused a commission in the RAF (to which he was already civilian consultant), when so many of his friends and colleagues were entering the Forces, showed courage. McIndoe believed that there was a proper course of action for treating the injured. He stated that ideally, continuous care should extend, directly or indirectly, from the moment of injury, to the point at which the injured person re-entered society – and beyond. He believed that these objectives had more chance of achievement if he remained a civilian working in conjunction with the armed forces. And so, whatever he had done before, from the time that he came to East Grinstead, he pursued these objectives quite without thought of the consequences to himself, using any means whatsoever which would further his aims. To him, the total needs of the patient were paramount.

He was 'difficult', he sought change not from any sense of rebellion as such but because the status quo so frequently did not produce the right answer. And similarly, it was entirely in this mood that he fought so bitterly and mercilessly to secure the abolition of the use of tannic acid, or any coagulation therapy, in the treatment of burns. And my goodness, how very many people have benefited from *that* battle over the last thirty-five years.

He spearheaded the efforts to make society – at least some society – aware of patients as individuals. While McIndoe foresaw that there might be individual problems, in some ways he never understood some of these problems. For to him, all patients were people and he never differentiated between people.

The Guinea Pigs recognised McIndoe's courage and responded to it. They saw this example and emulated it. And, interestingly, even in Queen Victoria Hospital itself, long after McIndoe's death, his way of doing things is still recognised by those who remember how it was. Russell Davies again:

> The basic demands which McIndoe made upon those who worked for him, or with him, were only two in number. First, that they were competent to do the job they set out to do. Second, that they gave a basic loyalty to the main objective, say, trying to secure the eventual return to society of a whole person.
>
> There were no exceptions, at any level among the hospital staff to these unspoken but continuing pressures. The cleaner was just expected to be a good cleaner, the nurse a good nurse, the anaesthetist a good anaesthetist. These pressures also led in their turn, in a quite unusual degree, to the continuous and not unfriendly examination of one's efforts and results with one's colleagues. One gossiped but constructively. This attitude for me was best caught many years later by a young Antipodean surgeon, working at East Grinstead for a year or so, who was standing quietly one evening at the back of a group of doctors in the Mess and looking reflectively at the half pint of beer in his hand. When asked what he was thinking about he said: 'You know this is a very odd hospital. All you talk about are your problems and failures. If I want to know about your successes, and there are plenty of those, then I have to go round the wards and seek them out for myself.'

Or around the world . . .

How would McIndoe, the perfectionist, the inexhaustible, have solved the dilemma facing the Club today? No one who didn't know him, no one even who isn't a Guinea Pig, a member of the most exclusive Club in the world, may make an intelligent guess at the answer. But, provided it didn't damage the Club, McIndoe's reputation was that of a man who couldn't resist the opportunity of building bridges between the Guinea Pigs and society, if it presented itself. Sometimes, he achieved it, even when it didn't present itself. . . .

It was Ben Bennions who described McIndoe as 'a god'. He said it without a trace of affectation, a sincere tribute to a man he revered. He said it while seated in the cockpit of a Tiger Moth he and Bill Maynall had flown from Yorkshire to give a demonstration of aerobatics at an October air display for the Shuttleworth Collection of aeroplanes.

Bennions was a happy man. Not long before, the Spitfire in which he'd been shot down in 1940 had been found and dug up, having been partly buried fifteen feet in the Sussex earth, six miles north of Brighton. It was now in a museum. He had heard that, to mark the event, a Sussex farmer had named a prize colt 'Bennion's Spitfire'. It had been a moment to savour.

Squadron Leader Bennions with easy familiarity made himself more comfortable in the cockpit. The sky was clear. The sun was bright. The day stretched ahead, long and promising.

Soon, this man with only one eye, who had been injured unto death, would be weaving once more his patterns in the sky, climbing like a bird, fluttering like a leaf, falling only to rise again. The message clear for all those who would read it:

> Up, up the long, delirious burning blue,
> I topped the windswept heights
>   where neither lark nor even eagle flew
> And whilst with high uplifting mind, I trod,
> The high untrespassed sanctity of space,
> I've put out my hand and touched the face
> Of God.

A man proud to have lived, rather than to have died, for his country; proud to be a Guinea Pig; proud to have met life face to face. Proud – and thankful.

Bibliography

BOOKS BY GUINEA PIG AUTHORS

Jo Capka: *Red Sky at Night* (Czechoslovakia)
Tom Gleave: *I Had a Row with a German*
Richard Hillary: *The Last Enemy*
Colin Hodgkinson: *Best Foot Forward*
Richard Pape: *Boldness Be My Friend*
Bill Simpson: *I Burned My Fingers*
              One of Our Pilots is Safe
Robert Wright: *Night Fighter*
              Years of Combat
              Dowding and the Battle of Britain

OTHER BOOKS ON THE GUINEA PIG CLUB

Edward Bishop: *The Guinea Pig Club*
E. J. Dennison: *A Cottage Hospital Grows Up*
Hugh McLeave: *McIndoe: Plastic Surgeon*
Leonard Moseley: *Faces From the Fire: a life of*
              Archibald McIndoe

The Guinea Pigs

J. Adamczyk
J. G. Adams
R. R. Adams
R. Adcock
H. Aldridge
J. A. Allard
J. Allaway
G. W. Allen
T. Allen
K. Allison
H. Anderson
I. Anderson
J. Anderson
J. A. Anderson
L. Anderson
J. R. Andrew
W. G. Anglin
J. P. Angold
R. I. Armstrong
J. D. Ashton
D. J. Aslin
R. L. R. Atcherley
M. R. Atherton
J. C. Atkinson

D. Bacon
R. Bagard
J. H. Bain
A. R. Ball
R. J. Ball
F. A. Ballentyne
A. J. Banham
V. Banks
W. D. Barber
J. S. Barker
A. A. Barrow
P. Barry
K. M. Base
G. E. Beauchamp

W. Begbie
J. Benbow
G. C. Bennett
G. H. Bennions
G. H. Bernier
N. E. Berrington-Pickett
L. E. Berryman
M. Biddle
J. Biel
F. Bielawski
H. A. C. Bird-Wilson
J. B. W. Birks
M. Bobitko
C. Boissonas
D. E. B. Bond
H. van D. Bonney
W. J. Bourn
A. C. Bowes
W. M. Bowyer
C. I. L. Boyd
G. P. Bradley
P. F. Branch
T. W. Brandon
K. Branston
C. Briggs
E. Bristow
R. Broadbent
E. Bronski
P. W. S. Brooke
R. H. Brooke
N. Brooks
J. Broughton
T. Brown
A. H. R. Browne
K. Browne
T. Browne
E. Brunskill
J. D. Bubb
J. W. Buckee

F. G. Buckle
H. W. Buckman
V. G. Bull
E. G. Buller
F. Bullock
G. Burrell
W. G. Burton
J. C. Butler
M. W. Buttler

L. Caddell
B. S. Cadman
E. A. Cain
L. Cameron
B. Campbell
C. Campbell
K. Cap
J. Capka
J. Carlier
E. L. Carlsen
R. Carnall
E. M. Cartwright
L. P. Catellier
E. Cecille
E. Chapman
M. Charbonneau
R. W. H. Charles
C. Chater
L. E. Chiswell
(Dr) R. G. Chitham
G. B. Clarke
J. R. Clarke
R. Clarkson
R. Cleland
J. Clifford
J. Colbert
A. T. Cole
J. Cole

L. P. H. Cole
G. Collier
R. Collin
R. Colyar
J. Condon
A. Cooke
C. Cooper
K. G. Cooper
W. Cooper
M. Coote
F. Coppock
A. Corpe
L. R. Corrigan
W. Cowham
J. W. Craig
S. Crampton
D. Crane
D. Crauford
H. R. Crombie
W. G. J. Cruickshank
J. Cummins
W. Cunningham
H. Curwain

G. Dakin
R. W. Dalkin
E. D. Dash
C. E. Davidson
K. Davidson
F. S. Davies
K. Davies
J. Davis
P. Davoud
E. J. Davy
F. G. Davy
R. D. F. Day
G. de Bruyn
E. J. de Lyon
F. J. Dean

L. Dean
K. B. L. Debenham
H. J. Dee
A. Deniall
T. Derenzy
Mohamed Dermerdash
F. Devers
W. Dewar
W. A. Douglas
G. Dove
O. Dove
E. A. Doyle
W. Doyle
A. S. Dredge
G. Dufort
G. Duncan
J. W. Duncan
R. D. Dunscombe

P. Edmond
G. Edmonds
W. Edmonston
G. D. Edwards
H. Edwards
A. Elkes
P. R. Ellis
Nedim Erakdogan
H. Ernst
J. Evans
J. Everett

H. Fairclough
F. Falkiner
G. R. Fawcett
E. Ferguson
J. Ferguson
G. Figuiere
S. G. Finnemore
K. Fisher
P. H. Fitz-Gerald
J. Fleming
G. Forbes
M. E. Forster
G. L. Fowler
R. P. Fowler
W. J. Foxley
R. A. Fraser
R. Fraser
R. G. Frederick
D. Freehorn
H. M. Friend

S. R. Gallop
R. Gambier-Parry
A. H. Gambling
T. A. Garne
R. Garvin
R. Gauvin
V. P. Gerald
F. G. Gibbs
K. Gilkes
J. Gillies
J. Gingles
G. B. Giradet
S. Given
T. P. Gleave
J. Glebocki
D. R. Glossop
N. W. Glover
W. Golding
C. E. Goodman
L. A. Goodson
J. F. Gourlay
R. Graham
A. Graveley
H. T. Green
J. Grill
J. Grudzien
J. N. Gunnis
E. Gwardiak

J. Haddock
L. Haines
D. Hall
K. Hall
N. D. Hallifax
F. Hanton
J. Harding
C. Harper
J. Harrington
W. W. Harris
L. R. W. Harrison
K. Harrop
P. R. Hart
D. Davey
F. R. Haslam
L. E. Hastings
A. J. Hawksworth
W. Heine
D. A. Helsby
A. J. Henderson
A. C. Henry
J. Heslop
G. Hewison

R. J. Hewitt
W. R. Hibbert
C. Hicks
D. Hicks
J. Hicks
W. J. Higgins
E. Hiley
J. P. Hill
N. Hill
W. Hill
R. H. Hillary
A. J. Hills
G. J. Hindley
C. Hitchcock
V. R. Hobbs
W. W. Hocken
C. G. S. Hodgkinson
R. Holdsworth
R. H. Holland
N. Holmes
N. P. C. Holmes
W. Holmes
J. Hood
J. Hooper
R. Houston
F. Hubbard
J. Hughes
J. D. E. Hughes
W. S. Humphreys
D. W. Hunt
C. O. Hunter
C. A. L. Hurry
G. W. Hutchinson
W. J. Hutchinson
R. H. J. Hyde

K. Intepe
N. L. Ireland
G. E. Jackson
J. W. F. Jacob
G. T. Jarman
J. Jarman
C. R. Jenkins
G. R. Johnston
B. Jones
I. M. Jones
I. W. Jones
J. S. Jones
O. Jones

F. Keene
J. Keep

J. H. F. Kemp
J. Kerr
F. P. King
B. Kingcome
J. Kirby
J. J. Knott
W. Knowles
W. P. Korwell
J. Koukall
E. |Krasnodebski
P. S. Kyd

E. LaCasse
N. Lambell
E. G. Lancaster
D. Lanctot
A. Lander
R. Lane
W. Lane
N. C. Langham-Hobart
A. Langland
S. Langley
G. Lawson
G. T. Lea
R. G. F. Lee
.S. M. Lee
T. M. Lee
A. Leitch
J. Lestanges
R. Leupp
E. J. Lever
J. Levi
B. Levin
W. H. Liddiard
E. S. Lightley
M. Lipsett
R. T. Lloyd
E. S. Lock
B. Loneon
S. Loosley
A. J. Lord
R. C. Lord
G. J. Lowe
J. Lowe
S. Lugg
D. M. Lunney
L. Lymburner

J. McBride
O. J. McCabe
R. C. McCallum
A. McConnell

S. MacCormac
G. McCully
T. McGovan
R. A. McGowan
B. McHolm
I. C. S. McIvor
T. D. McKeown
J. W. McLaughlin
A. C. H. Maclean
C. McLean
C. A. McLeod
D. McNally
D. C. McNeill
J. F. MacPhail
W. J. MacPherson
S. McQuillan
D. McTavish

R. Major
J. Mann
J. Marceau
J. Marcotte
C. Marjoram
J. Marshall
D. D. Martin
J. Martin
S. Martin
W. Martin
W. Martin
D. C. Marygold
R. M. Mathieson
J. Mathis
J. W. Maxwell
J. May
L. Melling
J. C. Melvill
W. R. Methven
J. Miles
N. E. Miles
W. H. Mills
B. Mitchell
S. R. Molivadas
E. G. S. Monk
J. F. Montgomery
M. Montpetit
O. G. Moore
F. S. Moores
J. Mordue
A. Morgan
I. C. A. Morris
H. J. Morson
M. H. Mounsden

G. D. Mufford
J. G. E. Munt

G. D. I. Neale
R. G. Nelson
A. Nesbitt
B. P. Nettleton
N. Newman
W. Newson
T. Nichols
N. Nisbet
J. Nivison
B. R. Noble
G. Noble
W. L. Noble
R. Noon-Ward
C. T. Norman
S. A. Noyes

J. B. O'Brien
D. O'Connell
K. O'Connor
H. Ogden
T. O'Halloran
E. Orchel
G. Orman
D. O'Sullivan
F. Overeijnder
E. Owen
B. Owen Smith

A. G. Page
R. B. Pape
H. E. Parratt
A. Paszkowski
R. H. Payne
T. J. Peach
E. G. Pearce
G. H. Pearce
R. E. Pearce
A. Pearson
H. Peel
J. K. Pelly
F. Penman
P. Pereuse
E. J. Perry
D. Petit
H. Phillips
L. Phillips
S. A. Piercy
D. Pike
J. Pitts

M. A. Platsko
T. A. Podbereski
E. Poole
J. Poole
K. L. Porter
R. Pretty
D. Price
B. Propas
A. Proudlove
D. M. Pryor
F. J. Quigley
I. MacP. Quilter
G. H. Raby
R. Ralston
H. J. Randall
R. F. G. Raphael
V. Rasumov
A. Ratajczak
J. Redekopp
J. Reece
C. G. Reynolds
G. Reynolds
J. Reynolds
S. Reynolds
C. Rhodes
D. B. Richardson
W. Richardson
J. Rickard
B. Ridding
F. T. Rix
E. J. Robbins
J. L. Roberson
E. D. Roberts
R. Roberts
T. J. Roberts
A. B. Robertson
J. H. Rogers
S. Round
A. Rowley
A. Royds
J. H. Russell
K. Russell

J. St John
J. F. M. Sampson
J. A. Sandeman-Allen
A. C. Saunders
R. T. Saunders
J. H. Schloesing
T. J. Scoffield
E. E. Scott
J. E. Scott

G. R. Scott-Farnie
D. R. Scrivens
R. Shallis
A. Shankland
W. Shankland
W. Simms
D. W. Simpson
J. H. Simpson
W. Simpson
J. A. Sims
A. Siska
L. Skoczylas
D. B. Smith
J. Smith
J. C. Smith
P. C. Smith
P. S. S. Smith
R. J. Smith
T. A. Smith
T. C. F. Smith
T. G. Smith
W. E. Smith
R. Smith-Barry
K. C. Smyth
A. B. Snelling
K. Snyder
(Dr) L. J. Somers
J. Southwell
G. L. Spackman
W. R. Speedie
B. Spooner
W. H. C. Spooner
J. W. C. Squire
J. Stafford
H. H. Standen
E. Stangryciuk
(E. Black)
W. M. Stanley
H. Stannus
A. Stansberg
D. Stephen
D. W. R. Stewart
H. J. Stickings
P. Stoker
C. Stone
F. Strickland
G. A. Stroud
G. Struthers
D. Stults
J. B. Sullivan
A. K. Summerson
P. W. Sutton

F. Swain
L. Syrett
M. Szafranski

R. Tait
W. Tanner
R. Tarling
H. Taubman
B. Taylor
D. Taylor
E. A. Taylor
G. F. Taylor
J. E. Taylor
D. F. Tebbit
A. G. Thomas
J. Thomas
D. L. Thompson
J. J. Thompson
J. M. V. Thompson
G. W. Tiplady
A. H. Tollemache
J. J. Toper

J. Tosh
W. Towers-Perkins
K. N. Townsend
J. K. Trask
J. R. Treagust
L. Tremblay
F. Truhlar
K. S. Tugwell
L. Tully
R. Turnbull
G. Turner

J. Varty
J. Verran
D. L. Vince
E. Vincent
R. Vivian
T. E. Voges

L. Wainwright
A. E. Wakley
C. Walker
T. C. Walshe

K. C. Warburton
C. G. A. Ward
H. C. Ward
W. C. Warman
P. Warren
C. R. Warwick
C. Watkins
F. Watkins
H. Watkins
J. T. Waterson
P. J. Weber
F. Webster
P. C. Weeks
P. H. V Wells
J. Welsh
J. Weston
F. V. Whale
B. G. Whalley
R. Wham
J. White
N. White
R. F. Whitehorn
M. W. E. Wild

C. Wilkes
L. R. Wilkins
G. Wilkinson
H. Williams
S. R. Williams
T. Williams
T. W. Williams
V. Willie
G. Wilson
H. Wilson
M. Wilton
J. J. Wishart
I. A. Wood
H. W. Woodward
P. A. S. Woodwark
A. Woolf
G. E. Wooley
F. G. Woollard
R. Worn
C. M. Wright
D. Wright
J. E. F. Wright
R. C. Wright

Guinea Pigs who fought in the Battle of Britain

J. A. Anderson	No. 253 Sqdn
D. J. Aslin	Nos 32 & 257 Sqdns
A. J. Banham	Nos 264 & 229 Sqdns
G. H. Bennions	No. 41 Sqdn
H. A. C. Bird-Wilson	No. 17 Sqdn
R. Carnall	No. 111 Sqdn
M. Coote	No. 600 Sqdn
R. D. F. Day	No. 141 Sqdn
K. B. L. Debenham	No. 151 Sqdn
A. S. Dredge	No. 253 Sqdn
R. D. Dunscombe	
J. Fleming (NZ)	No. 605 Sqdn
T. P. Gleave	No. 253 Sqdn
R. H. Hillary	No. 603 Sqdn
R. H. Holland	No. 92 Sqdn
D. W. Hunt	No. 257 Sqdn
C. A. L. Hurry	Nos 43 & 46 Sqdns
B. Kingcome	No. 92 Sqdn
J. Koukall (Czech)	No. 310 Sqdn
E. Krasnodebski (Polish)	No. 303 Sqdn
R. Lane	No. 43 Sqdn
N. C. Langham-Hobart	No. 73 Sqdn
E. S. Lock	No. 41 Sqdn
J. Lowe	No. 236 Sqdn
J. W. McLaughlin	No. 238 Sqdn
J. F. Macphail	No. 603 Sqdn
J. Mann	Nos 64 & 92 Sqdns
M. H. Mounsden	No. 56 Sqdn
B. R. Noble	No. 79 Sqdn
A. G. Page	No. 56 Sqdn
J. W. C. Squire	No. 64 Sqdn
W. Towers-Perkins	No. 238 Sqdn
G. Turner	No. 32 Sqdn
P. H. V. Wells	No. 249 Sqdn

Index

173